Contemplative Prayer for Today
Christian Meditation

Ernest E. Larkin, O.Carm.

Contemplative Prayer for Today
Christian Meditation

Published in Singapore 2007
by Medio Media
www.mediomedia.org
mmi@wccm.org

Cover Photograph by Björn Gaus, www.bg-fotodesign.com
Book Design by Subsonic Media, Germany, www.subsonicmedia.de

ISBN-13: 978-1-933182-55-1
ISBN-10: 1-933182-55-5

Medio Media is the publishing arm of The World Community for Christian Meditation

The World Community for Christian Meditation
International Centre, St Mark's, Myddelton Square,
London EC1R 1XX, UK
www.wccm.org

Printed in Singapore by
Stamford Press Pte Ltd

TABLE OF CONTENTS

The publication of this book has been supported by a generous grant from Father Ernest E. Larkin's brethren, the Carmelites of the Most Pure Heart of Mary Province

Preface

From 1969 to 1974 Dom John Main, an Irish Benedictine from Ealing Abbey in London, was headmaster of St. Anselm's preparatory school in Washington, D.C.. He had come to the United States to study theology at the Catholic University of America. This plan was changed by the request to take over the role of headmaster in the upscale school. He was an exceptionally talented man with broad experience in the diplomatic, legal and teaching fields. He accepted the invitation and this proved to be the right choice for him and the school. The role put him in contact with the wider public outside. A fortuitous visit from someone seeking spiritual direction led him to the discovery of the mantra as an early Christian prayer form in the teaching of John Cassian (360's-430's). The mantra is the repetition of a holy word or phrase as a way of prayer, and John Cassian regarded it highly as an effective method among the Desert Fathers and Mothers at the origin of Christian monasticism.

Before his entrance into the Benedictine monastery John Main had learned the practice of the mantra from a Hindu holy man, Swami Satyananda, and he found it eminently helpful. But his novice master thought differently and told the docile novice to discontinue it as something alien and foreign to Christian practice. He was to take up discursive meditation, the common form of mental prayer in religious groups at the time. This meant using his imagination and reason to think about and converse with God. He was obedient to the directive. It led to a long, ten-year spiritual desert. The mantra had nourished John Main for years, and now he was bereft of this source of grace. He was to take up the mantra again in God's time through the liberation he experienced in finding the mantra as a Christian form of prayer through the writings of John Cassian and the later medieval treatise on prayer called *The Cloud of Unknowing*. The seasoned monk felt called to return to the mantra as his way of prayer.

He proceeded to study the roots of Christian prayer in the New Testament and early church writers and came to realize that this way of praying was the earlier form of meditation in the church. Discursive meditation came later. Meditation with a mantra had a long history in the church in classic forms like the Jesus Prayer, popular for centuries among the orthodox monks on Mount Athos and a fixture in the Hesychast tradition. Father John chose to call his prayer Christian Meditation, mostly because he saw it as the original form of meditation in the western and eastern church, and also to distinguish it from Centering Prayer, which was growing rapidly in the English-speaking world. Christian Meditation is like Centering Prayer, but different, because the mantra is repeated throughout and not just occasionally. All these terms will be explained in detail as we proceed.

Christian Meditation as developed by John Main is the subject of this book. The reflections are the fruit of my own experience and study of Christian Meditation over the last twenty-five years. I write as an older Carmelite, in what my father used to call "the twilight years of life", and I am moved to write this book to share what I consider to be a great gift to the contemporary church. I have spent much of my adult life pursuing the topic of prayer as a desired personal goal and the object of theological study and research. My efforts have brought me to the door of the great treasure of Christian Meditation. My perspective is the Carmelite tradition of spirituality, which is the tradition I have tried to live and share over a lifetime. The book represents my studied conviction that this method of contemplative prayer can renew Christian life in the 21st century.

In the first chapter I present a brief account of my own entrance into Christian Meditation. Chapter two discusses the dynamics of this prayer; it is followed in chapter three by further illustrations about this from my own experience. Chapter four interfaces Carmelite spirituality and Christian Meditation, beginning with the early history of the Carmelite family and passing through its apogee in the great Carmelite doctors of the church, Teresa of Avila and John of the Cross, as well as in the lesser known but important Touraine Reform in 17th century France. In chapter five I will look at the "desert spirituality" at the root of both the Carmelite tradition and the teaching on Christian Meditation. Chapter six will look at how time in the desert relates to social action, apostolate or ministry. Chapter seven addresses a very Carmelite form of prayer called aspirations or aspiratory prayer which can be seen as a parallel teaching to that of Christian Meditation, like two branches of the same tree. Finally the last chapter treats mindfulness, another basic feature of all contemplative life and prayer.

Some of the material has already appeared in the *Review for Religious,* and in collections of essays. Chapter four was published in the book, *Carmelite Prayer, a Tradition for the 21st Century* (ed. Keith J. Egan, New York: Paulist Press, 2003) and chapter six in *The Ministry of Spirituality, volume 2* (ed. Robert Wicks, New York: Paulist Press, 2000) 267-280. I thank the editors and publishers of all these sources for their kind permission to reprint earlier versions of the chapters.

Finally I wish to thank the myriad persons who have assisted me directly or indirectly in my own formation and my understanding of contemplative prayer in general and Christian Meditation in particular. In the first place this means my own family of origin, both parents and siblings, and my adopted family that is the Carmelite Order. Then there is the whole panoply of teachers, colleagues, students, retreatants and friends too numerous to name, who have struggled with me to understand and to practice contemplative prayer. I thank Father Brian Johnstone for his introduction to this volume and I am grateful to all the other leaders and members of the World Community for Christian Meditation for keeping the torch burning bright, and especially Joanne Rapp, the local leader and founder of the Cornerstone Center for Contemplative Prayer in Phoenix, Arizona, who introduced me to Christian Meditation. I wish to mention and thank specifically the typist, Janet Morrissey, who guided the final copy to safe harbor through the sometimes unfriendly waters of the computer. The book is the distillation of the thoughts, desires and hopes of these many people, known and unknown, who have searched with me for the pearl of great price. May all of us continue to grow in the practice of contemplative prayer.

Ernest E. Larkin, O.Carm.

Some, perhaps many, who read this book, will have followed a path in prayer not unlike that described by Father Ernest Larkin. While few could claim to have been brought to the kind of prayer that he experienced, many will recognize familiar staging posts along the way. There were periods when we "white-knuckled" through the prescribed time, driven by zeal, but without the appropriate knowledge. Often, we showed up for meditation but left feeling that we had accomplished little in our rather confused meanderings, not realizing that "accomplishing" something was not the point. We may well have had similar practical questions, such as whether to encourage the imagination or not, whether to read, whether we should use the "word" up to a certain point and then let it go, or whether we should continue to say it. The answers to these questions must be personal ones and Father Larkin is clear on this: he is not offering a recipe book for a guaranteed successful meditation or contemplation.

The inner peace that comes with the gratuitous divine gift of contemplation radiates through the whole text. The author recounts his experience of many different "methods" but it is not his intention to prove that any one is necessarily better than another. His option for "Christian Meditation" follows from a sense of being personally called to this way. Those who have made a similar option will find in Larkin one who had gone before and who was at peace with the choice he made. His convictions will sustain their own option for Christian Meditation, but he is not a recruiter.

What one clearly learns in studying this book is that the quest for a deeper and more genuine experience of prayer is not for the dilettante. While Father Larkin experimented with different methods, he was not chopping and changing in response to whim, but pursuing a serious and exacting search for the path that God was offering him.

While these writings are in a sense a guide to practice, they also offer a deep theological analysis. This is not a matter of putting different spiritualities in a set of pigeon-holes as was the wont of some texts on spirituality. Father Larkin's concern is to interpret his own practice and experience in such a way as to relate it to the great traditions of the past. Words are not everything, but words help. As a scholar he introduces theological terms, for example in his elucidation of the differences between meditation and contemplation and the different senses that have been given to these words.

This enables us to understand the classic authors such as St. Teresa and St. John of the Cross and to enrich ourselves by reading their writings. At the same time, it assists us to understand the somewhat different usage of more recent authors, who may provide an account of prayer that is more amenable to our contemporary way of thinking.

Those who have already begun the way of Christian Meditation will find here a deeply satisfying interpretation of their own experience that will enable them to understand and appreciate it more fully. Those who have considered the possibility of beginning Christian Meditation will find a lucid and supportive description of this way of prayer and encouragement to take the step.

Brian Johnstone, C.Ss.R.
Professor of Moral Theology
Catholic University,
Washington D.C.

Chapter One

Three Ways to the Center

This introductory chapter is a bit of narrative theology, something of my personal journey over the last twenty-five or thirty years, trying to practice meditation and contemplation. My account begins in mid-stream of my religious life in the mid-seventies with the introduction into centering prayer. What do I mean by centering and centering prayer? These terms have become familiar and clearly defined today. It was not always so. Centering and centering prayer meant different things to different people in the 60s and 70s. An example is the article by Thomas E. Clarke, S.J. in the British publication, *The Way*, in 1977, entitled "Finding Grace at the Center". The title may be familiar because it named a collection of essays on centering prayer published by the Trappists in 1978 and again recently by the Ignatius Press. The original article was reprinted except for the last two pages, which in my opinion represented one of the chief contributions of the article at that time. I have a quarrel with the editors for their having deleted the pages and not indicating they had done so. Apparently they wanted to highlight the one form of centering prayer they were espousing in the booklet. So they dropped two other prayer forms that Clarke was presenting as ways to the center.

In the article Clarke presented a philosophical exposition of centering and then posed the question: how does one make the journey to the center? His answer was threefold. The first way was classical centering prayer, the way of dark faith, which proceeds beyond images and concepts and seeks to rest in the Indwelling God. The other two ways to the center used imagination and feelings; they were the prayer of images and fantasy and the practice of consciousness examen. All three were ways to the center, ways to dispose the soul for the great gift of contemplation. Together they offered a rich and broadly based prayer life. Teachers of centering prayer should have applauded the connecting of centering prayer with other forms of active prayer.

Centering prayer is contemplative in intent, but active in method as are all forms of meditation. It is not supposed to replace *lectio divina* or become one's total prayer life. As a spiritual exercise it deepens one's whole prayer life, for example animating liturgy and devotions.

Connecting the three ways put flesh and blood on centering prayer by acknowledging the role of the imagination and human effort in the process of centering. Clarke's paper stated a simple, even obvious fact, namely, that the search for contemplation, especially in beginnings, is not an abstract act; it invokes images and thoughts, even while it strives to get beyond them. All three ways converge to the center. This was a welcome reminder in the early days of centering prayer. I remember how the insight thrilled me. I talked about the distinctions with Father John Kane, a Redemptorist who founded a contemplative house of prayer in Tucson, Arizona. We both agreed that the article was a breakthrough, because it made room for the imagination at least in the beginnings of contemplative prayer. One did not have to force the journey away from images, trying too hard to empty our minds. Clarke's article contextualized the search for contemplation, showing classic centering prayer as one way to contemplation, a good way, but not the only way.

Prayer and Imagination

The three ways of centering were a significant help to me. Two years earlier, in 1975, I had made a 30-day Ignatian retreat and came away with the resolution to spend an hour each morning in mental prayer. I was faithful to the hour, but I lacked method. My prayer was amorphous. I read and reflected, I pondered, mused, made affections and resolutions. I also centered and sat for long periods of silence. But there was no particular order in my pondering. After two years of struggle to be faithful to the hour without a clear methodology, my prayer had become dry and difficult. I "white-knuckled" my prayer, holding on to the bench to fill out the hour. All this may have been a species of the *determinada determinacion* of Teresa of Avila, but it was probably closer to the *zelus sine scientia corruit* of St. Bernard. "Zeal without knowledge destroys." How long could I hold on? Only the grace of God kept me from giving up on the hour.

My efforts in the hour were the same as my practice in the two daily periods of formal meditation in my Carmelite community over the years. These two periods were shorter, usually a half-hour each, and I was able to handle them, though somewhat haphazardly. Because they were amorphous, I subsequently looked on them disparagingly. I thought I had wasted a lot of time in my mental prayer. I do not think that way now. I have come to take a more benign view. I agree with Woody Allen that 95 percent of life as well as of prayer is showing up. If we are there, putting in time with the Lord, the Lord will do the rest. We should not exaggerate the role of method but it certainly helps. The three ways of Tom Clarke supplied a format for my contemplative prayer. I would do twenty minutes of classical centering prayer, twenty minutes of reflection on the day's readings, and then after Mass twenty minutes of journaling. I did not characterize the imaginative parts of my prayer – the biblical meditation and consciousness examen – as contemplative, but I saw them as part of my pursuit of contemplation.

At this time I made a study of the prayer of St. Teresa of Avila in her early pre-mystical years to determine how she employed the imagination in her beginning contemplative prayer.[1] She later called this "practice of prayer" active recollection. Her prayer used her innate gift of imagination. It was active in form but contemplative in goal, since her whole effort was to rest in the deep, personal realization of the Divine Indwelling. This was her whole prayer. Teresa called it "re-presenting Christ within". Commentators sometimes incorrectly interpret this phrase to mean the imaginative recall of some mystery in Christ's life, for example, an image of Christ at the scourging at the pillar. The imaginative recall is part of the prayer, but not its heart, since the recall is only the refocusing of the person in moments of wandering. The remembrance of an image from the passion serves the same function as the holy word in centering prayer. The holy word does not detract from the contemplative character of centering prayer any more than the image in active recollection.

Teresa's active recollection, which can rightly be called centering prayer, was both apophatic, i.e., beyond imagining and thinking, and kataphatic, i.e., with a role for the imagination. These insights into Teresa's prayer confirmed Clarke's suggestion and allowed me to accept a minor but real role for the imagination in my own practice and shaped my daily mental prayer for some fifteen years. I did not, however, practice it twice daily as was specified by "Contemplative Outreach" under the leadership of Thomas Keating. I now realize the two periods of 20 to 30 minutes, morning and evening, are essential for the discipline of centering prayer. These periods are catalysts for one's prayer life. They are like workouts in a physical health regimen and their role is to bring one's life to a deeper level in one's spirit. The outcome is the goal of contemplation in Carmelite terminology.

The Move to Christian Meditation

In the mid-1990s I switched my prayer practice to Christian Meditation, a similar but different form of centering developed by John Main, an Irish Benedictine from England. I did so, mainly because I was not satisfied with *my* practice of centering prayer. I felt called to take the step beyond imagination and for this I felt the need to focus more strongly on the repetition of a prayer phrase to the exclusion of everything else – at least at the times of meditation. Christian Meditation is promoted by the World Community for Christian Meditation, headed by Laurence Freeman, O.S.B. The difference between Centering Prayer's use of "the holy word" and Christian Meditation's use of "the mantra" specifies these two forms of contemplative prayer. The holy word expresses the will of the person to rest quietly, silently in the Lord. The mantra, on the other hand, carries the prayer. It has a sacramental quality, an outward sign of inner grace, both a means and an end.

The differences are subtle, the practice is very similar. The nuances of their respective teachings represent different traditions and expressions of apophatic prayer. In Centering Prayer the 'word' expresses our 'intention' to rest in God, it is a way to come to our center. Once we are centered and resting in God, the 'word' can be let go of. For Christian Meditation the 'mantra' is a focus of 'attention': We say it until we can no longer say it, until all self-consciousness is lost in the silence of God. I personally felt called to the discipline of a continuous repetition of the prayer word. It was a personal journey but one that enabled me to be faithful to the two times of meditation a day that both teachings recommend.

My personal preference for Christian Meditation is not a condemnation of centering prayer; the same fruits and benefits are available in both forms. Christian Meditation repeats the mantra, usually the biblical prayer "ma-ra-na-tha", which means "Come Lord", from the beginning to the end of the prayer. The holy word, on the other hand, is not repeated continuously but only as needed to renew the consent to the Divine Presence. John Main does not tire of saying that the mantra is the prayer. It creates the silence that is emptiness and openness before God, the silence that invites the Divine Presence. However both mantra and prayer word are disciplines that nurture the beatitude of the gospel: "Blessed are the pure in heart, for they will see God." (Matt 5:8) Both traditions are valid.

As a Carmelite I feel there is a closer affinity between Centering Prayer and Teresa of Avila and between Christian Meditation and John of the Cross. I base this opinion on the similarity between active recollection and centering prayer, and the absolutes of the *Nada* and the *Todo* in John with the call to kenosis or self-emptying in Christian Mediation. In the final analysis the two approaches are more alike than different. For this reason I have studied them together and emphasized what is common to them. The leadership in the two movements works closely together and sees their ministries as parallel. One example of this close collaboration is a prayer center in Phoenix called the Cornerstone, which has been sponsored by both movements, sharing the same space in a former convent in the Carmelite parish of St. Agnes. The Cornerstone Center has offered programs that are sometimes common to both groups and sometimes specific to one of them.

Prayer without Images

I have come to see Christian Meditation as a companion piece, a "how-to" addition to the teaching of St. John of the Cross on the passage from discursive meditation to contemplation. This area is one of his specialties. The transition from one state to the other can be difficult if not traumatic. Discursive meditation for John is a rational activity but it can also use the imagination, feelings and emotions. It is active and self-directed. Contemplation, non-discursive meditation, is passive. It is receptive of the gift of the love that comes from God. It is the practice of the presence of God. The transition from one state to the other can be disturbing. Beginning contemplation may look like a step backward, even total loss, a drying up of thought, imagination, and emotional feelings. The old way of active prayer is no longer appealing or even possible, and the new way of contemplation is not self-evident. The experience is the passive dark night of the senses. It is a great grace, but easily mistaken and open to misunderstanding. John gives his famous three signs to authenticate the state as well as detailed instruction on the conduct to be followed.

In discursive meditation one deals with concrete, individual acts, striving to remove the bad ones and to promote good ones. One is analyzing, evaluating, making choices and resolutions. The soul is like a windowpane,

St. John says, and the work of such reflection is to remove the smudges of bad habits and replace them with acts and habits that are bright with the light of Christ. The light of Christ is faith. The windowpane is lit up by a faith-motivated activity. Over time the window becomes basically clear and the soul purified in its choices. The light of faith shines through with fullness, simplicity and wholeness. This is the light of contemplation. The light is always there, John of the Cross says. It is part of the state of grace. The perception of the light, however, is dependent on being rid of self-centered, selfish habits. John writes as follows:

> *"This light is never lacking to the soul, but because of creature forms and veils that weigh on it and cover it, the light is never infused. If individuals would eliminate these impediments and veils and live in pure nakedness and poverty of spirit their soul in its simplicity and purity would be immediately transformed into simple and pure Wisdom, the Son of God." Ascent 2.15.4*

The way of contemplation is self-awareness of this new state of being in grace through the infusion of light and love. One simply opens the eyes and sees and basks in the love and presence of God. At first there will be a going back and forth between prayer using thought, imagination and will and, on the other hand, the prayer of silence. John of the Cross gives detailed advice on how to recognize the times for the one or the other; when to pray actively and when to rest in the contemplative light and love. His teaching is renowned for its clarity and effectiveness for spiritual direction and retains its place in the life of every budding contemplative. But it is a complicated teaching. Along comes John Main who sees meditation and contemplation in continuity with each other and as one process. The active 'work' of saying the mantra is the way we let go and realize that it is not us who are praying but, as St.Paul says, "the Spirit is praying within us in groans that cannot be put into words".

The prayer or discipline of Christian Meditation is one dynamic that begins with the mantra and stays with it through multiple experiences of God's love. Contemplation is the awareness of Abba's love for me, who am bonded with the Son in the love of the Holy Spirit. The contemplative grows in the appreciation of this love and gets in touch in ever deeper degrees with the knowledge and love that the Trinity showers on the world. There is *communio, koinonia*, participation in the reality of God and God's creation. This communion is unitive knowledge, of subject and object mutually inhering in each other. It is not dualistic knowledge, from the outside, leaving subject and object apart from one another. It is not any particular psychological experience. There is at-oneness, a "common union" or communion, in which the Trinity and the human being enter into what Teresa of Avila called "two things becoming one".

Communion is the ontological reality, contemplation adds awareness and attention. Not every experience of Christian Meditation is infused contemplation such as John of the Cross has in mind. But every experience is communion and eventually will bring the fullness of contemplation. The commitment to Christian Meditation is a commitment to a way of life. The way is always the same; it is the way of the mantra from beginning to end. The goal of the prayer is without limits. One stops saying the mantra only when one is reduced to silence. These are moments of special grace that John of the Cross calls "oblivion". (*Living Flame 3.35*) One resumes saying the mantra as soon as the silence is recognized, because that is the sign that the special mystical grace has passed.

John Main's program is one of utter simplicity. He does not stress, though he may acknowledge in theory, the abstract differences between active prayer and contemplation or the different degrees of contemplation. But he treats them as one spiritual practice and says explicitly that meditation, meditative prayer, contemplation and contemplative prayer are all synonyms.[2] There is no need to measure where one is on the path. The important thing is to grow in purity of heart and receptivity to divine grace. The journey is the same in both John of the Cross and John Main, but it is described from different viewpoints. The older John presents objective theology in the manner of the scholastics; the younger John has made the turn to the subject and his exposition is experiential and practical. Laurence Freeman remarks that John Main's purpose was to start people on the journey and let experience of the prayer teach the rest. The one task proposed is the mantra. The mantra does not deal with obstacles one by one or even supply building blocks for a spiritual edifice. It sweeps the window clean in one fell swoop by silencing the mind and emptying it of its contents. The silence makes room for the Spirit to take over. "Be", says John Main, "and you are in the Spirit".[3]

The Spirit is already there with Father and Son in the Divine Indwelling. If the soul is silent and receptive, the Spirit will pray there beyond images and thoughts, in sighs too deep for words. (Rom 8:26) The Spirit will do this, because the soul is open and ready, and God wants that mutual indwelling even more than the soul who is sincerely seeking God. John Main's simple method frees the person so that the life of the Trinity can come alive and be actualized. When there is space and freedom, the meditator is caught up in the prayer of Jesus. That prayer is the one and only prayer in the world because of the Incarnation, because the Spirit of truth is the love between Father and Son that envelops all of creation. Faithful meditators tune into that universal salvific love.

The journey with the Son to the Father will traverse the stages of Teresa of Avila and John of the Cross. Christian Meditation can be the vehicle, the discipline to get one going and to help one stay on the path. These are astounding claims for Christian Meditation. Their justification is the beatitude: "Blessed are the pure in heart, for they will see God." (Matt 5:8) The silence of the mantra produces the purity of heart, and the reward of purity of heart is the love of God, of people, and of the world found in the gift of contemplation. How does silence accomplish this twofold task? By allowing one to escape from the false self, by placing one beyond the toils of ego and the world it creates, by freeing one from the imprisonment of false desires. This healing produces purity of heart. The new freedom allows one to go deeper into the spirit, the domain of the Trinity. The reality of this state is primary and comes before awareness and appreciation. The reality is called *communio* or participation in the life of God; the awareness is contemplation. The Spirit will give us contemplation when we are ready.

Contemplation is thus the outcome of faithful practice of the mantra. Contemplation is the life of God received, the backdrop and engine of one's whole spiritual life. It is the life that animates one's community relationships, one's ministry and one's prayer life. The short definition is the realization of God's love for us, "the love of God poured forth in our hearts by the Holy Spirit, who is given us." (Rom 5:5) Contemplation is the outcome of a faithful life. It means claiming what was there from the beginning. It is the *Abba* experience of Jesus. In his human life Jesus was filled with the Father's presence and love. Certain events like the Baptism or the Transfiguration were climactic experiences of that love. But Jesus abided in that love always. He looked out upon the world bathed in the Father's love. He was the "beloved son" and in him the reign of God was established on the earth. That reign is the kingdom of God's presence and love. It is the Resurrection experience. It fills the world with the grandeur of God. Christian Meditation promises this contemplation. Each practice will not necessarily bring forth a recognizable, reflexive experience of that love. But every exercise will put one a little more in touch with it and will be an experience of communion, of *koinonia*, of participation in that love. Transformation is taking place, slowly, incrementally, and the Christian is being formed in "the Wisdom of God, the Son of God, in whom we live and move and have our being".

Endnotes

1 "Teresa of Avila and Centering Prayer," *Carmelite Studies* (Washington, D.C.:ICS, 1984) 203-209.
2 Talks on Meditation (Montreal, 1979) 10.
3 *John Main, Essential Writings* (ed. Laurence Freeman, Maryknoll, N.Y., Orbis Books, 2002) 105.

Chapter Two

What Is Christian Meditation?

"Christian Meditation" is capitalized, because the title is a specific form of meditation developed by John Main, a Benedictine from England (d.1982), based on the teaching of a Swami friend in Malaya, on the fourteenth century treatise on contemplative prayer called *The Cloud of Unknowing* and on the earlier monastic conferences of John Cassian (d.432). Cassian recorded the practices of the Desert Fathers and Mothers in Egypt and Palestine. John Main took one such practice, "monologistic prayer," which is the repetition of a short phrase from Scripture as a mantra, drew on *The Cloud* authors recommendation of the use of "one word" in prayer, and turned it into the daily discipline of Christian Meditation. A movement called the World Community for Christian Meditation came later to promote and coordinate this prayer. Its headquarters are in London under the leadership of Dom Laurence Freeman, O.S.B., one of John Main's original disciples. This chapter will present the main features of the contemplative prayer form.

The standard description of the "how to" of Christian Meditation comes from John Main himself and appears in many of his writings:

> *Sit down. Sit still and upright. Close your eyes lightly. Sit relaxed but alert. Silently, interiorly, begin to say a single word. We recommend the prayer-phrase maranatha. Recite it as four syllables of equal length. Listen to it as you say it, gently but continuously. Do not think or imagine anything – spiritual or otherwise. If thoughts or images come, these are distractions at the time of meditation, so keep returning to simply saying the word. Meditate each morning and evening for between twenty and thirty minutes.*[1]

Christian Meditation is a daily prayer of silent and loving presence to the Indwelling God. Its distinguishing feature is the mantra, the word "ma-ra-na-tha", which means "Come, Lord", repeated throughout the prayer. The meditative prayer is contemplative, i.e. it seeks to get beyond rational thinking and multiple affections and to enter the realm of the spirit, where deep quiet of mind and heart can be fostered. The discipline represents a democratization of contemplative prayer. In past eras this kind of prayer was restricted to advanced souls who were unable to pray discursively, often because they had exhausted the potential of reflection and affective colloquy and were reduced to silence before God. The new form is active prayer, chosen on one's own initiative and pursued as a human effort under ordinary grace. It is properly called meditation and not contemplation, but meditation in a non-discursive form. There is no movement from point to point, no elaborate reflection or affections and resolutions, but simply the invocation of the mantra and utter attention. It is an older, classic form of meditation found in the desert and in early monasticism, including the early Carmelite hermits on Mt. Carmel in the 13th century. It is like centering prayer, but different, since it repeats the mantra throughout, whereas Centering Prayer uses the holy word only as needed. Both forms are creative methods of getting started and continuing a contemplative practice.

Some experience in prayer is presumed but not emphasized. The method is simple. The practitioner is to sit still, upright but not stiff, relaxed but attentive, letting preoccupations fall to the side. Breathing automatically slows down and goes deeper into the diaphragm. In a composed state the mantra, ma-ra-na-tha, is sounded interiorly. The Aramaic rather than an English translation, "Come, Lord", is preferred, just as it is recorded at the end of 1 Corinthians and the Book of Revelation. There is no effort to unpack the meaning. Its role is to draw and occupy the mind, away from the person's own agenda, thus helping the one praying to attend to the moment. The mantra silences egoistic concerns and creates an emptiness that invites the presence of God. It silences what John Main calls the chattering monkeys in the psyche. All thinking and emoting are unwelcome, even holy thoughts and desires. All distractions are momentarily noted and allowed to pass by.

The one praying is dwelling deep down, as if at the bottom of a river, and distractions are like surface vessels passing overhead. Their presence is recognized and ignored. The prayer is saying the mantra, listening to it, letting it absorb the attention, as one falls deeper into silence. In the silence there is communion with the Beloved as a reality, not in some image or reflection, not in any tangible or recognizable way, but simply in touching the truth and reality. Communion is participation in the being who one is, and that being is one with the Holy Trinity. Communion is only awareness of one's new being in Christ. It involves no particular psychological experience. Often it seems as if nothing is happening, nothing except a new reality, the great gift of indwelling and inter-penetrating with God.

Meditation and Contemplation

Since the time of St. Teresa of Avila and St. John of the Cross the terminology in mental prayer has been fairly well fixed within the two basic categories of meditation and contemplation. Meditation is an active reaching out to God with one's own thinking and willing, and contemplation is God reaching out to the person with the gift of love and presence. Meditation in the West is usually discursive, that is, it moves from point to point and act to act in a rational process that employs all one's faculties under the influence of ordinary grace. *Lectio divina,* which means holy reading, usually of Scripture, is a typical example. It has four steps. It begins with reading and is followed by reflection and then praying to God in affections, petitions, and resolutions. The process culminates in contemplation or quiet resting in God.

A second kind of meditation, a style popular in the East and once common and presently being renewed in the West, is non-discursive. It is contemplative meditation. If it were placed in the schema of the four acts of *lectio divina,* it would come as the conclusion of the third act of prayer and at the threshold of contemplation. It is knocking at the door of contemplation. Or, more accurately, is like opening the door for Jesus, who stands outside at the gate and seeks entry into the inner room of the heart. (Rev 3:20) There is mutuality here; both the Lord and the seeker knock at the door and wait to be invited in to have supper together. Each wishes to give the self to the other. The divine gift of love is contemplation, not necessarily in the strict sense of infused contemplation, but as God reaching out in love. The meditator receives the gift and rejoices in the new life originally received in baptism and now actualized by grace. God is looking for his beloved more than the beloved is looking for God. They meet in the dwelling place of God which is the human spirit. This contemplation is the outcome of *lectio divina.* For John Main this experience emerges out of the meditation, and is not rigidly distinct from the meditation, since for him meditation, contemplative prayer, and contemplation are interchangeable terms, all synonyms of each other. This is the older, monastic usage of the terms.

Contemplation does have a specific content as the goal of all meditative processes and, in fact, the heart of all Christian vocations. Its purest form is infused contemplation, which is a gratuitous, unmerited gift of loving knowledge of God, in the language of John of the Cross, "an inflowing of God into the soul". But contemplation is also the outcome and residue of a faithful prayer life, and then it is called active or acquired contemplation. Whether acquired or infused, the point of the gift is always the same: it is to know the ineffable love of God. Contemplation means to be in love with God, a privilege that is given to each person coming into the world, a gift to be interiorized, appropriated, and subjectively experienced through a life of progressive self-transcendence.[2] In whatever way the grace of contemplation comes, it is God freely giving himself in love and presence to one of his spiritual creatures.

All Christian life seeks union with Christ in knowledge and love. Contemplation is the name of that reality. It is no one particular act or experience, but a new state of being, the transformation that God works in us by the gift of his love. The contemplative realizes that love; first in the ontological way of a renewed humanity, and then in the consciousness of that new 'being in Christ'. The original gift is God's love for the person. The love creates a new, dynamic ordering of one's whole life that finds expression in a full Christian life, not only in prayer, but in human relationships and ministry. In short it is a new life in Christ. Contemplation is the kingdom of God achieved; it is the life of grace come to maturity. The consciousness and awareness of God's love triggers a return of love. But the specific essence of contemplation is the awareness of the original gift.

The identification of contemplation with God's prior love is the thesis of an article by Gunter Benker, O.Carm., who defines contemplation as being in touch with God's love for us, rather than with our love for God.[3] In our relationship with God the initiative always belongs to God. The apostle John says: "Love, then, consists in this: not that we have loved God, but that he has loved us." (1 John 4:10) "It was not you who chose me", Jesus said at the Last Supper, "it was I who chose you." (John 15:16) When Therese of Lisieux sees her vocation "to be love at the heart of the church", she is describing her response to God's prior love. Her life project is to carry out that love in word and deed in her world, to spread "the love of God poured forth in our hearts by the Holy Spirit, who is given us." (Rom 5:5) Contemplation is the reversal of the sin of our first parents and our own failures. Sin rejects God's love and brings on enmity and brokenness. Grace restores the original design of God, and its fullness is the state of contemplation. Acceptance or rejection of God's love spells the difference. The human vocation of all peoples is to leave alienation in favor of the oneness of all things in God.

In this perspective one can see why Jesus in his human life was the perfect contemplative. His every action, his every choice expressed the Abba experience, the realization of the Father's love for him and for all creation. There were moments of special revelation of the Father's love, as at his baptism in the Jordan, when he heard the words: "You are my beloved son. On you my favor rests." (Mk 1:11) From those insights he saw the world bathed in the Father's love. That made him see everything in a divine light and in the Father's will. He recognized evil, of course, but he saw the divine hand beneath the surface of things and the long-term good in all human events. So he loved unconditionally, the good as well as the bad, saints and sinners alike.

How different were the clouded minds of Adam and Eve after their rejection of God's love. The serpent promised them a supposed blessing for eating the forbidden fruit, to know both good and evil. The "blessing" was a curse. After the fall they were divided creatures, approving the good but attracted to the evil. (Rom 7:15) They were slaves to destructive forces within and around them. Having lost their innocence they lived in a dualistic world, and they were no match for temptation and sin. Paul laments: "Who can free me from this body under the power of death?" (Rom 7:24) The answer: the grace of Jesus Christ our Lord.

Heirs of original sin, people come into the world as divided creatures, gifted with the love of God, being in love with God as Bernard Lonergan says, but victimized by ignorance and concupiscence. It could have been different. Humanity could have been born in integrity and seeing only good. Instead people come into the world alienated, perceiving their fellow human beings as threats, competitors, possible enemies and challenges to their freedom.

They have some good inclinations, but they are prone to the false gods of "consumption, luxury, money, efficiency, power, perfection, and symbiotic relationships." [4] We need to be healed of these idolatrous dependencies by the *metanoia* offered by Jesus so as to see the world with God's eyes, the eyes of unconditional love. To the extent that we rise above ourselves and interiorize the gift of God's love we will have reached contemplation. We will be full participants in God's life and love. The contemplative does not judge; she does not pick and choose; she loves like Jesus and "unto the end". (John 13.1).

The Father's love has been given freely in the Holy Spirit and received as members of Christ's Body. The gifts are there waiting to happen. They are aspects of divine love, and they are appropriated in proportion to the measure of self-transcendence in knowing and loving that the person has reached. In that measure people participate in God's life and see as God sees. The work of self-transcendence embraces this whole spiritual journey. Everything in our lives contributes, not only our prayer life, but also the way we share life in community and ministry. Our choices have the immediate goal of hollowing us out for divine life, achieving emptiness (*kenosis*) in order to participate in fullness *(pleroma)* in imitation of Jesus Christ, who "emptied himself, accepting even death; death on a cross! Because of this God highly exalted him and gave him the name above every other name, Jesus Christ as Lord". (Phil 2:7,11) The heart of our imitation of Jesus Christ is "to know him and the power of his resurrection and the fellowship of his sufferings". (Phil 3:10)

We have the same double objective as Jesus, emptiness and fullness. We will be visiting this theme many times in the course of this book[5]. The practical question is how to accomplish the twofold goals. The long answer is the whole spiritual adventure, the array of multiple tasks and exercises in the spiritual life. The short answer and the specific offering of this book is Christian Meditation. Christian Meditation addresses the two aspects. It is only one discipline in the journey to God, but it can and does function as the centerpiece of all one's endeavors, animating and energizing all the practices of the spiritual life.

One such practice is *lectio divina*, the holy reading and pondering of God's word, especially in the Scriptures. God's word is nourishment for Christian life. Even the most advanced contemplative can still benefit from the Holy Scriptures, not to mention the liturgy and other standard devotions. Christian Meditation is a way of the heart that gives new life to the search for God in Scripture. *Lectio divina* and Christian Meditation are complementary; they assist each other and work together for the progress of the Christian life. We now take a look at the inter-relationship of these two 'ways of prayer'.

Lectio Divina

In *lectio divina* we approach God with our reason, using imagination and feelings to stir up faith and love. The four acts of *lectio* –reading (*lectio*), reflection (*meditatio*), praying (*oratio*) and contemplation (*contemplatio*) – can be followed in order or any one of them can become the focus of the moment. The first three acts are active, rational, self-initiated, the work of *ratio* or reason; the fourth is passive, the receptive work of *intellectus* or understanding. The first three acts address Christ-for-us, who is the Savior redeeming us and calling us forth. The fourth act shifts gears and relates to Christ-in-us, the Christ become present within through the transformation of our being in him. In the first three acts we take hold of Christ in order to grow in configuration to him. This transformation begins in baptism and grows through the practice of the Christian life, especially through the life of prayer. Once transformed and configured in his image we experience ourselves united with Christ and related to God the Father and the Holy Spirit in a participated Trinitarian life. At one and the same time we are in touch with ourselves and with Christ, because the two inter-penetrate each other in mystical unity.

Lectio divina is supposed to end in an awareness of oneness with God. The process uncovers and reveals God, and we end up in silence like Mary of Bethany sitting at the feet of Jesus. Too often, however, this goal is short-circuited and the whole time is spent on busy prayer. The contemplative dimension goes begging. Energetic prayer is commendable enough, but it should not short-change "the better part". (Luke 10:42). The moments of quiet resting in God are an anticipation of even better things to come. The desire to insure those moments has been one of the reasons for the search for a more explicit way of contemplative prayer. The search undertaken by the Trappists at Spencer, Massachusetts in the 1970s resulted in the discovery of Centering Prayer. Shortly thereafter John Main developed the close relative of Christian Meditation.

Lectio divina was the setting for Centering Prayer, as indeed it is for Christian Meditation. It is the counterpoint of these two contemplative prayer forms. Both point and counterpoint are complementary and enlighten each other, and neither side can be dissolved into the other. *Lectio divina* thrived in the Middle Ages and served the monks and the nuns well, filling the time between the liturgical offices and other duties. Its purpose was to nourish the mind and heart with holy thoughts and desires. In the 16th and 17th centuries the cultural shifts called for new methods of mental prayer to counteract the encroachments and distractions of the busier environments of town and city that were emerging in Europe. The new methods of meditation were more structured, more detailed, and more imaginative than the freewheeling and flexible *lectio divina*. These methods of meditation have been standard fare in religious communities and serious seekers of God throughout modern times.

Lectio divina suffered fragmentation and the four inter-locking stepping stones were separated and became degrees in the life of prayer. The reading became spiritual reading, not exactly a prayer form, and generally regarded as less salutary than mental prayer, whose first degree was discursive meditation. This exercise became the *sine qua non* of a serious religious existence. Affective prayer (the *oratio* of *lectio divina*) came next, and finally a simple, contemplative stance such as the prayer of simplicity, which was one long act of love of God, or the prayer of faith, which was silent attention beyond discourse, or even acquired contemplation, in which the sense of God's presence was seen as the fruit of previous struggles. Infused contemplation was a special gift that could not be tracked as part of every journey.

Practitioners were advised to stay within the form proper to their growth and they were not to anticipate a higher way. Discursive meditation was the staple. Affective prayer was an advanced form of meditation, pursuing affections instead of thinking. A third stage was ordinary or active contemplation. In the anti-mystical temper of the recent past, including the first half of the 20th century, infused contemplation was deemed a rarity, a special gift not to be presumed. Louis Hertling, a Jesuit professor of ascetical theology in the Gregorian University in Rome, opined that there would likely be one person in a large community who would be gifted with this grace. Theologians argued about its precise nature and its relationship to sanctity. For some it was the normal outgrowth of an ordinary prayer life of loving faith and the crown of spiritual development. For others infused contemplation was a special experience of God's presence, an extraordinary gift, and not necessary for sanctity. This question was hotly debated for centuries.

However one understands the nature of infused contemplation, authentic contemplation of whatever origin always includes a profound sense of God's love. It is a different category from para-mystical phenomena like stigmata, visions, locutions and the like. There is less concern in writers today about these distinctions of form and substance in mental prayer and the classification of different stages. Once it was insistent teaching that one should pray actively as long as one was able to do so. This is the strong teaching of John of the Cross. One did not arbitrarily choose to practice contemplative prayer, even the so-called acquired type, before the famous three signs validated the choice, namely, an inability to reflect discursively, aversion to all particular and sensible forms, and, withal, a burning desire for God.

There is less insistence today. In any case Christian Meditation is not in violation of the traditional advice, since it involves the active work of saying the mantra. For this to open to infused contemplation, passivity before God's grace, a steady commitment to the practice must be in place. Christian Meditation carries the same teaching as John of the Cross; not to anticipate the silence but to continue saying the prayer word "until one can no longer say it". The first three stages of Lectio are concentrated in the saying of the mantra which, as the simplest form of active 'acquired' contemplation, disposes one for the gift of infused grace. The emptiness of the single word will lead to the fullness of Divine presence for the Kingdom of God belongs to those who are poor in spirit.

Recently *lectio divina* has regained its popularity as the preferred method of discursive meditation. It has made a comeback generally, and not just in Benedictine circles where it has probably always flourished, partly because of the retrieval of the bible as the primary text of devotion and theology for Catholic Christians in the wake of Vatican II, and partly because it promises and provides a contemplative experience. The bible has become once again the primary prayer book of the Christian, and Catholics again search the holy book for ways to experience God at prayer.

Dynamics of the Practice

Christian Meditation does not replace *lectio divina,* but it puts fiber into this form and the entire prayer life. Christian Meditation is more contemplative than *lectio,* because it is explicitly contemplative, eschewing thinking and even formulated acts of the affections. The mantra is calculated to serve silence and stillness. The mantra has no magic power but is sacramental, a sign charged with God's presence. It comes from the earliest forms of Christian monasticism where biblical *haga* and meditating on the law of the Lord meant the conscious repetition of a word from Scripture. The Scriptural *ma-ra-na-tha* was taken over in Christian Meditation, not as an object for reflection, but as a device to free up the attention from one's own agenda in favor of the experience of silence and of one's own poverty. The emptiness is the seed-bed for communion with God

The mantra functions as sound and not as an intelligible word, as is well stated in the following testimony of a young mother who practices this meditation:

> *You concentrate on that one sound [of the mantra] – not it's meaning - in order to still the mind. There are moments when there is only sound; only rest; an experience of love, wholeness, gift. But in general – while aware of guarding against wanting success or even progress in the practice – just keeping the sound present for half an hour and watching the movement of the mind is a tiny experience of detachment, a holding of your preoccupations at arm's length, a tiny look away from yourself. It is a moment quiet enough to turn to God and – as Mother Teresa put it – 'to listen to God listening to me.'*[6]

The mantra's work is to detach oneself from ego and be liberated for God. Christian Meditation is contemplative from start to finish. It is rightly called meditation, because it is applying one's resources to the work of saying the mantra from start to finish, gently brushing off distractions, and cultivating a generalized attention. The contemplative mode comes from the desire to enter into silence and to rest in the stillness of God.

Contemplative prayer as wordless and imageless is an innovation in prayer practice for many adult Christians of this time. They are used to formulas or else chatty conversation with God. Christian Meditation is interested only in the journey inward. The mantra clears the mind, gets beyond thinking, and takes one from the head to the heart. The mantra is not repeated mindlessly, neither is it an object of analysis. It is recited attentively, savoring its sound interiorly, its richness and its promise, and letting it remove one from the anxieties of the moment. The person stands at the gate, watching and waiting, at attention, listening but hearing nothing, since the listening is to silence. The silence is not day-dreaming but focused and intentional. The pray-er is present to everything and to nothing before the mystery of God. There are many mantric prayers in the Catholic tradition, notably, rosaries and litanies and antiphonal repetitions. There is also the Jesus Prayer, the signature prayer of eastern Christianity, and it is structured the same way as Christian Meditation. Here the mantra is "Lord Jesus Christ, Son of God, have mercy on me, a sinner." Both Christian Meditation and the Jesus Prayer seek to know Christ, not just to know about him. Both seek to enter the deeper regions of the soul, to be present there with one's whole being, and to have a person-to-person contact with God. Christian Meditation uses the mantra as the instrument of purification and illumination. Its function is to steer one away from the free-floating, undisciplined curiosity of the ego, to spare the person the aimless meanderings of the mind. All activity that is about "forms and figures," to use John of the Cross' phrase, all that is particular and fragmented is to be transcended in favor of "a long, loving look at the real".

Teilhard de Chardin has the following moving description of the journey into interiority:

> *And so, for the first time in my life perhaps (although I am supposed to meditate each day!) I took the lamp and, leaving the zone of everyday occupations and relationships where every-*

thing seems clear, I went down into my inmost self, to the deep abyss whence I feel dimly that my power of action emanates. But as I moved further and further away from the conventional certainties by which social life is superficially illuminated, I became aware that I was losing contact with myself. At each step of the descent a new person was disclosed...And when I had to stop my exploration because the path faded from beneath my steps, I found a bottomless abyss at my feet, and out of it came – arising I know not from where – the current which I dare to call my life.[7]

This is a good example of a meditative practice that is contemplative in nature. Christian Meditation is a similar journey inward, and the mantra is the lamp that lights the way.

Being on the Way

A journey has three phases that correspond to the point of departure, the journey itself, and the goal. These intervals can also apply to the journey of the prayer. The point of departure is a distracted mind and self-serving spirit. The inner journey is the gradual renewal of mind and heart through growth in self-knowledge and loving knowledge of God. The goal is finding the center, the dwelling place of God, and remaining there in blissful union. The stages are not linear, but spiral, and we pass through them, revisiting the three points over and over again. Their relationship, however, is progressive as befits the image of journey. We begin on the outer level of our lives, where we are often superficial, jejune, and perfunctory. We flit from topic to topic, waste time with trivia, and are subject to diverse and unpredictable feelings. How can we bring order out of this chaos? How can we organize our intentional activity to allow us to live more meaningfully and to love more truly? The answer is the mantra, and saying it is the first step of Christian Meditation.

We employ the mantra to quiet ourselves down, to heal our errant desires, and lead us into peace. Saying the mantra from beginning to end of the prayer will be the first step and a more difficult one than we might imagine. Faithfully enunciated the mantra will gradually help us to take our attention off ourselves and free us from disturbing appetites. The mantra is a discipline that weans us away from confusion and unifies us in our inner being and our outer commitment to God. The first step transports us into a new mentality that abandons images and desires in favor of silence. The mantra is not a mechanical droning, but a focused, and holistic practice of attention. Its faithful repetition is the first step but a big one in the conversion enterprise. The discipline takes patience and perseverance, not to mention faith and love. It promises harmony and peace in our souls.

Once the attentive repetition of the mantra is secure, we enter the second stage of expanding our self-knowledge and God-knowledge. This second moment is the long haul, the process of interior renovation. The operative field here is no longer our superficial consciousness, but what is below the surface and often only vaguely noticed. The mantra will penetrate unexamined and unconscious parts of the psyche and allow them to surface their contents. In calming the mind and creating silence the mantra makes us more aware of our devious egos and lets the truth come out in an atmosphere favorable to self-acceptance. Personality traits, patterns of thinking, value systems, and character limitations will emerge. Some of these things are already known or half-known in one way or another, but perhaps without responsible owning of their implications or effects. We are engaged in mining the unconscious, and the self-disclosures will happen in gradual or in sudden ways with different emotional resonances. In the time of the prayer itself we simply know and own them and let them pass by. We humbly accept ourselves, thereby taking a first step toward healing. A more comprehensive therapy might be addressed outside the prayer, for example, a twelve-step program. In the prayer time we do not analyze or work out a strategy to deal with our weaknesses. We simply accept them in the loving presence of God.

Most of the new insights will probably be new realizations, real knowledge in Newman's sense that goes beyond the notional ideas that do not engage us. The new self-knowledge may need to be examined in a rational fashion and with the help of a counselor or spiritual director. Because these disclosures can be disconcerting and threatening and even overwhelming to the individual, it is good practice to have a skilled companion or community to accompany us on the contemplative walk, not each time we meditate, but as an available consultant. If we are discouraged over our prayer the support of others on the way, in a weekly meditation group, can encourage us. In an extreme case when dread or panic takes over at prayer one may need to seek advice from a spiritual companion or professional counselor. The role of a community like The World Community for Christian Meditation and Contemplative Outreach is to provide the teaching, guidance, friendship and recourses that can keep us 'on the way'. Difficult as it may seem it is a path that many around the world are walking, and many throughout history have walked before. We always meditate as part of a community and a tradition.

At the same time there is also a new perception of God in Christian Meditation. The knowledge here is not new information, but new appreciation. God becomes more real, more attractive, more mysterious, and especially more loving. Prayer does not increase one's speculative knowledge of God. It clarifies and personalizes the infinite love of God. Contemplative knowledge is knowing God by way of love. The quality of this knowing is illustrated in the intuitive embrace of a mother for a suffering child as compared with the clinical examination of the physician. God becomes more personal as Friend or Companion, as Beloved, as Abba, Jesus, or Holy Spirit. God becomes a person. This increase in loving knowledge of God is the primary contribution of Christian Meditation. The mantra, repeated in faith and love, begins to express this new relationship. It is like a friend we turn to in time of need and joy, like a secret language we share only with our beloved, a way of evoking the divine presence in all the circumstances of our life. "God is love," St. John the Apostle writes, and the way of the mantra is the royal road of love. It is the direct route to the heart of God.

The twofold growth in self-knowledge and the loving knowledge of God is the promise offered by Christian Meditation. This two-pronged reward establishes purity of heart, which brings with it the gift of contemplation, according to the beatitude, "Blessed are the pure in heart, for they will see God." (Mt 5:8) These conditions, purification and intimacy with God, are the foundational structures of religious life, according to John Cassian. They are also the blueprint for every spiritual enterprise. They sum up the *yin* and the *yang*, the negative and positive poles, of every vocation in the church. Purification is the way, and contemplation the goal of every journey of faith.

John Cassian offers some helpful commentary on how "monologistic prayer" can accomplish so much.[8] How does the repetition of a Scriptural phrase accomplish so sublime an achievement? The overall goal of all prayer in John Cassian's view is "continual prayer," the prayer without ceasing of the gospel (Luke 18:1). Prayer is a way to living in the presence of God constantly. In Cassian's view the only prayer capable of that lofty a goal is "pure prayer", the wordless and imageless prayer of contemplation. Such prayer is the "prayer of fire", so-called because it is inflamed with ecstatic love. Monologistic prayer is the direct route to continual prayer, to pure prayer, and to the prayer of fire, and all three are the same one reality. Yet the question remains: how does the mantra achieve this high state? It does so by inspiring an all-round holy life, and more directly by teaching the lessons of poverty and humility, the purity of heart that is the underpinning and the measure of all union with God. The faithful praying of the mantra, not only in formal meditation but also throughout the day, will lead to the mountain of God.

John of the Cross is equally optimistic and offers a theological interpretation of the dynamic of purity of heart and contemplation. In two short paragraphs he presents what looks like an updating of John Cassian. He first develops the thought that the light of contemplation comes with baptism and "is never lacking to the soul, but because of creature forms and veils that weigh on it and cover it, the light is never infused".[9] Because of our blockages we are untransparent to grace. The removal of these obstacles, says John, brings about poverty of spirit, purity of heart. As soon as this happens, the soul "would then be immediately transformed into simple and pure Wisdom, the Son of God." The Christ-for-us becomes the Christ-within-us, now mystically one with our humanity and experienced in participative unity.

The person addressed by John of the Cross in this chapter is someone who has gone beyond discursive meditation and can no longer use "forms and figures" in their prayer. These persons are to "remain in God's presence with loving attention and a tranquil intellect, even though they seem to themselves to be idle. For little by little and very soon the divine calm and peace with a wondrous sublime knowledge of God, enveloped in divine love, will be infused into their souls."[10] Do not John's words apply as well to those who choose to follow the discipline of emptying their minds of reasoning and cultivate silent presence before the indwelling God? John remarked earlier that the infusion of the light would have been received and perceived from the beginning, except for the "creatures and veils" of attachments that cloud the soul. These "creatures and veils" are removed through the self-emptying of Christian Meditation and the result will be the same inbreaking of God of which John speaks.

When does the third stage of pure and fiery prayer occur? When does the light of contemplation shine in the soul? The gift is there all along, as John of the Cross has just said, and it will come to expression in proportion to the emptiness achieved. God comes in when the door is open. The love of God is palpable, consciously perceived, and pervasive in the person's whole being, when the obstacles are removed. The goal is transformation, the cost is, in T.S. Eliot's words, "not less than everything". Christian Meditation offers a manageable way to reach this high destination.

Endnotes

1 *The Inner Christ* (London: Darton, Longman and Todd, 1987) V.
2 *Method in Theology* (New York: Herder and Herder, 1972) 105,237-244.
3 "Contemplation –the Heart of the Carmelite Charism," in *Carmelite Formation, Proceedings of the International Programme for Carmelite Formators* (eds. Alexander Vella and Gunter Benker, Rome: General Curia of the Carmelite Order, 2002) 37-52.
4 Ibid, 39
5 This twofold project is developed at length especially in Chapter Four on the Carmelite way to God.
6 Juliette Lange, "A Mantra for All Mothers," *Tablet* 25 September 2004
7 *The Divine Milieu* (tr. Bernard Wall, New York: Harper and Row, 1960) 76-77
8 *John Cassian: The Conferences* (tr. Boniface Hanley, O.P., New York; Paulist Press 1997) *Ninth and Tenth Conferences*, esp. 9.2,1-2 (329-330); 9, 15,2 (339); 10,11,6 (385).
9 *Ascent* 2.15,4
10 *Ascent* 2.15,4-5

Chapter Three

The Experience of Christian Meditation

It is one thing to theorize about Christian Meditation and another to experience it. Experience is not transferable, but personal accounts can evoke some part of the original reality. The present chapter proposes to share some experiences of the prayer. The author will attempt to describe his own experiences over the past several years and in particular during an intensive practice in a retreat of five weeks at the Camaldolese Hermitage in Big Sur, California in fall 2000. The chapter is his own interpretation of what went on in the five or six periods devoted to Christian Meditation each day. First there is a review of some of the dynamics of this prayer and then descriptions of the personal experience. These accounts were read critically by some experts in Christian Meditation, and they were approved as authentic expressions of the method.

The Mantra

People in all walks of life all over the globe have practiced Christian Meditation successfully. Where does it get its power to empty the soul and encounter the divine presence? Not from some magic power of the mantra. For John Main the mantra was a way of faith. The mantra in Christian usage is "an aspiration of the heart," to borrow a phrase from St. Therese of Lisieux.[1] The mantra is spoken by the mind, but it is expressive of the heart, here meaning the whole person. The heart, in its biblical meaning, is the deepest part of ourselves and the center of the person.

The mantra creates emptiness and fullness within ourselves to the extent that the heart is one and not divided. This means that the mantra's effectiveness is in direct proportion to the degree of personal integration and the intensity of engagement and attention in the prayer. The mantra expresses the surrender of one's whole being to God. But of course we surrender only as much of ourselves as we possess. That is the measure of our freedom. The saints invest their whole being, because they are undivided and enjoy real poverty of spirit. Beginners do the best they can. They cultivate Christian Meditation as an act of renunciation of their own thinking and preferences to create a hollowness within for God to fill. This is the dynamic of emptiness and fullness in mantric prayer.

"Ma-ra-na-tha" is a Scriptural greeting (1 Cor 16:22), and it means "Come, Lord." In this prayer it is put forward, not as an explicit petition, but as a way of focusing one's attention on the God within. The mantra articulates a single-pointed, non-discursive attention to the Gracious Mystery dwelling in the depths of one's being. Discursive thoughts or images or sentiments are unwelcome intrusions, even if they are holy ones. Stillness is the goal; firstly physical stillness, and then total and single-minded attention. The mantra is the expression of a committed mind that desires to let go of everything except the mantra itself in order to be wide open to the divine presence. The mantra is a new language for loving God and receiving God's love.

Human openness and the divine presence thus stand in direct ratio. God comes, according to John of the Cross, where there is an opening.[2] The mantra is a prayer to let go of everything but itself, thus moving the person beyond lesser interests into the region of the spirit. God is spirit and dwells in our spirit and center beyond the imagination or reason. The journey to God leaves all else behind and, again in the imagery of John of the Cross, it moves by the feet of faith and love into the heart of God.[3] Thus the passage ideally is leaving everything for the Everything that is God. The mantra is an instrument for appropriating the first beatitude: "Blessed are the poor in spirit, the kingdom of God is theirs." The mantra is a prayer for the coming of the kingdom. John Main insisted that it is more a discipline than a technique.

Detachment is key. In the monastic tradition detachment often goes by the name of purity of heart, a biblical phrase that is less open to misinterpretation than detachment, which in ordinary usage means apathy or not caring. Spiritual detachment is caring that is just right, that chooses the right things, in the right measure, and for the right reasons. Detached people are free, integrated, and rooted in God in all their loves. They are open to the truth, because the word of God is the basis for their every decision. They act out of their true selves and are not slaves of their false selves. Biblical faith is the best synonym for detachment.

Silence as the Way to Poverty and Presence

The language of Christian Meditation is silence; the mantra is a discipline of selfless attention that brings self-centered thought to silence. This is a silence that is loving and open. Open to others and to the great Other, God, who paradoxically dwells within us. God is Love, as St John says. Shortly before she died, St. Therese of Lisieux lay in the convent infirmary unable to sleep. Her sister Celine looked in on her and asked her what she was doing. "I am praying," she responded. "And what are you saying to God?" Celine asked. "I am saying nothing. I am loving him."[4] Christian Meditation is loving God.

All prayer is conversation with God, though not necessarily with words. In Christian Meditation the language on both sides is silence. God's side of the conversation, his word, according to John of the Cross, is the conferral of grace. "The language of God," John says, "is the effects he produces in our souls."[5] The effects are sharing God's life, also called communion, and the mutual indwelling takes place in silence. The more silence the better. There is a place for words in our conversation with God, but not at the time of Christian Meditation. Again St. John of the Cross puts the superiority of silence in strong terms: "The language God best hears is silent love."[6] Meister Eckhart offers a similar adage: "There is nothing so much like God as silence.[7]

The mantra is said silently, interiorly, from beginning to end to cultivate interior silence; it ceases only when one is reduced to absolute silence and is can no longer articulate the phrase. At this point our mind is in union with God. 'Saying the mantra' resumed when one notices personal thinking is breaking the silence.[8] The mantra is said with "selfless attention." This is more than the half-awareness of ordinary, discursive consciousness. It is non-discursive, one-pointed attention to the exclusion of everything else.[9] The energies of one's mind and heart are concentrated on the mantra as the path to God. As our consciousness becomes more familiar with the sound of the mantra over time it becomes rooted in us; we move from saying it, to sounding it, to listening to it with ever-deeper attention. When it finally disappears self-consciousness itself is lost in the silence of God.

The goal of Christian Meditation is "the other side of silence," or "pure prayer," the fruit of detachment or purity of heart. In John of the Cross 'poverty of spirit' and contemplation are practically the same thing.[10] So are purity of heart and the fullness of the Christian life in the teaching of John Cassian, who sees these two related as the means and the end, the way and the goal, the immediate aim (*skopos*) and the final objective (*telos*) of the spiritual life. In John Cassian's teaching, under God's grace, these two elements are united.[11]

The recitation of the mantra is a confession of weakness, a gesture of dependence, a confession of lack of personal resources to effect a relationship with God. It is a signal to God that the words of Romans 8:26 are taken seriously: "The Spirit too helps us in our weakness, for we do not know how to pray as we ought; but the Spirit himself makes intercession for us with groanings that cannot be expressed in speech." In Christian Meditation there is no search for the meaning of "ma-ra-na-tha," no theologizing about it, but only its articulation as a gesture, a communication beyond words. The goal of the prayer is person-to-person contact, which is more than just thinking about

God or one's self. This is the level of contemplative, non-discursive activity.

Ordinarily Christian Meditation does not end in an empirical or sensorial experience of the Divine Indwelling. Such mystical gifts are possible, but they are not the immediate intent of the prayer. Meditators settle for silence; they accept in faith that they are moving into a deeper level of relationship with God. They believe they are in touch with God, though there is seldom proof of this in their immediate experience. There is simply silence. Discernment of spirits will help one interpret the affective moods that accompany or follow the prayer. The proof of the prayer is its aftermath, the good attitudes and the good works it produces.

Theory and Practice

John Main says that the mantra carries the prayer and there is nothing else, no other supports, no other strategies or devices. Yet all prayer is contact with God, and even mantric prayer must keep God as the ultimate horizon. I now interpret the mantra to be the direct focus, and God the oblique focus of the prayer, something like central vision (in this case the mantra) and the peripheral one (here God). God is not an object of thought during the time of the meditation but there is a growing sense that it is in God that we "live and move and have our being", as St Paul says. With this caveat I have found the simple recitation of the mantra effective, especially if I am centered when I begin. I experience its gentle power to free me up and bring me to a deeper place. In the prayer I do not advert to the purpose of self-emptying and/or presence. I simply engage the mantra, which starves other interests and moves me to be quiet and at home with the Lord.

I take this experience as normative for Christian Meditation. I began with it and I have returned to it after a detour of some experimentation with figures or images, which will be described in the next section of this chapter. I consider the first mode the normative form of the prayer. Here is one example from my journal of November 8, 2001:

> *My second meditation this morning was again a consolation. I just said the mantra. I experienced it, not just as clearing the decks, as it were, and brushing away all thoughts and preoccupations but boring inward deeper and deeper into the fathomless depths of the God who is totally other, beyond any and all thoughts about him. I was carried to that center, which was never reached, and I dwelt there, happy to be in touch with God in the emptiness. He is the emptiness and I touch him in faith (and not in a communicable experience) when I say the mantra. Alleluia.*

There was no engagement of the imagination and thought in the above prayer, though there was a sense of moving inward. Sometimes I was dimly aware of the Spirit praying within me, as in the following account:

> *This morning [November 1] after a wonderful sleep of eight hours, I rose at 4:45 a.m., made a fire, then immediately did my meditation. It was wonderful. I stayed put till I looked at the clock and found I had spent a full half hour with my prayer and a sense of God's presence. I had a sense that the Spirit was praying Christ's prayer within me. The Spirit was saying "Maranatha" and opening my heart to the divine presence.*

The images in the above accounts were spare and merely accessory, but they were a help to me early in the retreat. So was the sense of praying with my whole being and not just my voice or mind. The following reflection (November 1) illustrates these aspects:

> *Contemplative prayer is person to person, whole to whole. So I try to create an attitude or atmosphere of bringing my whole self to the gracious Mystery. I don't think of the Father or of Jesus I simply bring*

myself to the Gracious Mystery. Sitting down I briefly ask God to enter and bestow the grace of union. I try to keep this request in a non-discursive mode. Then I listen with my whole being as if intuitively:

I believe now that the deliberate imaginings I engaged in were a foreign element in Christian Meditation, especially if they are extended into the time of the meditation. I justified the intrusion of the imagination by telling myself that I was not working the images, only recalling them; they provided a "sense" or a "feel" or a background for my saying the mantra. I knew I should stay with the mantra alone. Eventually I was able to dispense with these imaginative structures. My typical practice is recorded in the following entries on November 3:

My first meditation this morning was from 5:30 to 6:00 a.m. I simply said the mantra slowly, attentively, synchronized with my breathing (which was not very deep). I was aware that I was praying and, therefore, in the presence of God. I experienced the poverty of the whole procedure, namely, that I was a beggar with no thoughts or feelings and in the presence of God. I felt my emptiness was the underside of fullness... There was no particular experience of God, just a sense of love and gratitude. In my second attempt, after returning to my room from Lauds and a detour to pick up muffins in the kitchen, I started the mantra and did not advert to the geography of my soul. I simply began the mantra as the instrument of self-emptying. The Spirit is there in the darkness, apophatically. I do not expect any sensation about God. I know in faith God is present.

Sitting erect in a chair with my back straight prepares me to get into a pattern of deep breathing, which is a sign of the life force within. In the East this life force or energy is called *ki* or *chi*, and, as William Johnston says, correct posture allows it "to flow freely through the body [and] ...through the top of the head to the outermost reaches of the universe and down through the spine and the anus to the inmost depths of the earth."[12] A simple recall of these factors seems to facilitate my prayer. I connect my posture and breathing with the mantra and all three together express the movement into the depths. I synchronize my breathing with the four syllables of the mantra, breathing in with "ma-" and out with "ra-," in with "na-" and out with "tha." John Main does not regard control of the breathing as essential to his method. I have found it helpful. Sometimes I think of the syllables as aspirations, a breathing forth of love as aspirative prayer, an addition to Christian Meditation which will be discussed at length in chapter seven.

Equally or more important in becoming acclimated to the simple recitation of the mantra was my appropriation of a non-dualistic theology about the contemplative experience. My faith had always told me that the life of grace was a participation in the life of God. My faith and my theology told me that God was not an object separated from me, but that I lived in God and God lived in me. I did not realize till the retreat and reading some of the work of one of the Camaldolese monks, Bruno Barnhart,[13] that the experience of this participation was not the cognition of an object out there, but an experience of intersubjectivity; Christ-for-us becomes Christ-in-us, one with us. It is the experience of the reality of God in a non-dualistic, unitive way called communion.

John Main writes beautifully on the theology of the Divine Indwelling; he describes the dynamic life of the Trinity, Father, Son, and Holy Spirit, going on within us. When we meditate, he says, we are participants in that life. We are not outside observers; we are caught up in the divine processions and are experiencing God. The Spirit is praying within us and the prayer is the one prayer of Jesus, in which all authentic prayer participates. Our prayer places us in the stream of love between Father and Son.

Do we recognize the persons and the divine mysteries when we do Christian Meditation? No, not in objective, communicable terms. The consciousness here is different. It is unitive and participative, present because we are one with God and participating in God's very life. Knowledge of God is like the knowledge we have of ourselves. The original knowledge of ourselves is non-reflexive. When we make ourselves the object of a thinking process, we have knowledge that is once removed from experience.[14] It is the same when we think *about* God and use words for God. By learning, study, observation and analysis we can know useful things *about* God and *about* ourselves. Meditation teaches us simply to accept the gift of our being and to realize that "we live and move and have our being in God", as St Paul said. This is the primary knowledge; being who we are by participating in the being of God. This experiential knowledge has no image of self or God mediated by thought. It is the dynamic fruit of mutual presence.

In participative or unitive knowledge we experience the divine mysteries as part of ourselves; they are incarnate in us by the "continuous incarnation" of the life of grace. This is the kind of knowledge St. Paul refers to when he prays that we might "know God and the power of his resurrection and the fellowship of his suffering." (Phil 3:10) This experiential knowledge is ineffable (beyond words and speech) and apophatic (beyond images). If we talk about it at all, we do so in metaphors and analogies taken from our experience in other realms. When we use words like Father, Son and Holy Spirit for God, we are talking about God in human concepts. The knowledge is true, but reduced to a figurative level of discourse. The experience of God in Christian Meditation is apophatic and ineffable; it is the awesome experience of the reality of God. But we cannot communicate it even to ourselves without domesticating it. It is a unique knowledge and love that are possible, because God has gifted us with oneness with himself.

The mystery of God is present in us beyond all names, metaphors, and analogies. God is both transcendent (dwelling in inaccessible light) and immanent (the source of our being). To live that transcendence and immanence is to find our own divine-humanity and become 'a new creation in Christ', a child of God. This is an incredible gift; it is rightly called mystery. Grace transforms me into Christ, so that "the life I live is not my own; Christ is living in me." (Gal 2:20) God himself is outside our ken and beyond language. The mystics put this in strong language by saying that God is Nada, Nothing, nothing in the language of creation, nothing in ordinary human experience. But by grace and love this God has become one of us in Jesus Christ and we are one with him in his risen body. This reality we can and do experience, immediately, subjectively, but incommunicably, just like the direct experience of ourselves. It is the experience of our new selves. Language fails here; silence is its only expression. Christian Meditation is silence and stillness before the Lord.

The mantra is language in the service of silence. The mantra points, the silence experiences God. The work of meditation is like peeling away the rind of an orange so as to taste the fruit within. In "kataphatic" prayer God is perceived in concepts and words, as for instance in the recitation of the psalms, but in contemplative prayer God dwells in the silence. I see nothing, I touch nothing, I understand nothing, I surrender myself. In union with Christ I trust my whole being onto God. Yet in this surrender I am met by the love of another who's self-gift is infinitely greater than mine. Meditation is that mutual gift where we find the self we left behind in the love of the other. Like St Paul we can say; "I live by faith in the Son of God, who loved me and gave himself for me." (Gal 2.20)

In Christian Meditation I do not permit the imagination or the discursive reason to intrude. I note, but I do not stop in thoughts or sentiments, even pious affections. I do not enter into them, because my task is silent love.

I proceed with the mantra, which allows me to be one-pointed, to empty my soul and give silent attention to God. The mantra is the whole prayer. Repeated in love and faith it peels the hard rind of the ego, the conditioned self, away, and reveals the sweet fruit of our true self within. This stripping of the conditioned self is purity of heart and contemplation in some form. The mantra incarnates the beatitude; "Blessed are the pure of heart, for they shall see God". (Matt 5.8) More than that, by participation, they shall *be* God.That every beatitude is first and foremost a be-attitude. This is the guiding principle of the monastic life, according to John Cassian. The monastic life is structured to develop purity of heart, and its goal is to see God but seeing God is not from the outside, as if I am watching God as an object outside myself. The meditator looks at God from within. This seeing is participation and communion.[15] The East understands this kind of knowledge more easily than the West, because the East is expert in the principle of *advaita* or non-dualism. The knower becomes "one same thing" with the known, to borrow Teresa of Avila's strong definition of union. The meditator is absorbed in Christ, but without losing his or her own identity. It is the way of silence and stillness.

Here is a last description of 'perceived silence' from my retreat diary, November 5 [16]:

> *I am happy that I am able to go beyond the twenty minutes. Part of the reason is saying the mantra in a relaxed manner, like deep breathing that is now natural and without concentrated effort. The breath is soft and it merges into the effect of the mantra, namely, the still place where God dwells. There is no sensation Presence.*
> *The mantra occupies the attention, keeps the mind busy in a most simple way, and the intuitive self, the region of the spirit, comes to life. I am happy just being there with the Lord, saying nothing, expressing no sentiments, just silent and still.*

The following is another account two days later:

> *I feel my Christian Meditation is stabilized now. I enter into myself, drop down to the lowest level at the core of my being, and I stay there. That is all. It is so simple. The mantra leads me there by eliminating other concerns, all thoughts, feelings and preoccupations. I enter within and keep going back to the mantra, all the time cultivating a sense of surrender, of playful love for my God. Praised be God and Our Lord Jesus Christ.*

Endnotes

1 *Story of a Soul* (tr. John Clarke, O.C.D., Washington: Institute of Carmelite Studies, 1975) 242
2 St. John of the Cross, *Living Flame of Love,* 1.9; 3.46
3 St. John of the Cross, *Spiritual Canticle,* 1.11
4 Victor Sion, *Chemin de priere avec Therese de Lisieux* (Paris:Cerf, 1993) 63
5 *Living Flame* 1.7
6 *Spiritual Sentences and Maxims* in *The Works of St. John of the Cross* (tr. E. Allison Peers, Westminster, Md.:Newman Press, 1953, III, 232, n.53.d
7 Reference in Eckhart's works not known to the writer.
8 John Main, *The Inner Christ,* 103
9 For a clear presentation of discursive and non-discursive attention see Philip Novak, "The Dynamics of Attention: Core of the Contemplative Way," in *Studies in Formative Spirituality,* 5 (1984) 65-80
10 *Ascent of Mt. Carmel,* 2.15.4; *Spiritual Canticle* 10.5
11 *Conferences* 1.4-8
12 *Arise, My Love* (Maryknoll, N.Y.: Orbis, 2000) 5
13 I am grateful for discussions with Father Bruno about non-dualistic thinking and reading his excellent unpublished paper, entitled "Christian Self-Understanding in the Light of the East: New Birth and Unitive Consciousness." This paper has since been published in *Purity of Heart and Contemplation* (ed Bruno Barnhart and Joseph Wong, New York: Continuum 2001) 291-308.
14 Denys Turner, in *The Darkness of God* (New York:Cambridge University Press, 1995) 87-89, analyses this teaching of St. Augustine.
15 Laurence Freeman writes in the *Christian Meditation International Newsletter,* September, 2000, page 3 that; "For the desert monks the first goal of life seen as a spiritual process was to reach purity of heart. This gospel term and Beatitude of Jesus is echoed in all traditions. It empowers us to "see God", not as an object of perception or as an abstract concept or as a fantasy projection of wish fulfillment, but in and as reality. Seeing God, according to the Christian tradition, is the true

meaning of life and to reach this goal is to find the happiness that lies at the spiritual core of every human act and desire. The vision of God is an experience of communion rather than observation".

16 The fact that the silence is perceived shows there is still a self-consciousness left to objectify it into an 'experience'. Journaling is helpful but can only take us to the threshold of silence. I offer my own experience in the hope that it might be a help to others 'on the way'.

Chapter Four

The Carmelite Tradition and Christian Meditation

The question of this chapter is how Christian Meditation relates to the Carmelite tradition on contemplative prayer. The whole book is mindful of this question: How can the Carmelite teachings on prayer illuminate the contemporary practice of Christian Meditation, and vice versa. The author has been formed in the Carmelite tradition, so he has a personal bias of judging new movements by their compatibility with the tradition of Carmel. Is Christian Meditation in continuity with the tradition or is it something new and different, even contradictory to the received teaching of the past? The short answer is a strong vote of confidence in John Main's method. Christian Meditation fits beautifully into the Carmelite system and in many ways it is a re-statement of its perennial teaching.

The Carmelite tradition is an old one which begins in the 13th century. Its charism is prayer and contemplation. The first Carmelites were heirs of the Desert Fathers and Mothers, whose wisdom was preserved by John Cassian, whom we have cited several times in these pages. He collected the teachings and practice of the deserts of Egypt and published his findings in two volumes called The Conferences and The Institutes.[1] The original Carmelites were hermits, full-time contemplatives, dwelling in cells and caves on Mount Carmel in northern Israel. They were westerners and belonged to the Latin Kingdom in the Holy Land. Their life plan, called a "formula of life," was given to them some time between 1206 and 1214 by the Latin patriarch, Albert Avogadro, who served in that capacity in that period. It was a pastiche of biblical texts and set down a simple way of life for the hermits. They were to live in separate cells apart from each other and to come together for meals, the recitation of psalms, weekly chapter meetings and daily Eucharist. Prayer and community were the twin pillars of their life.

After the conquest of the Holy Land by the Saracens they were forced to emigrate to Europe and eventually to become mendicant friars. The formula gradually became the canonical Rule of St. Albert with final approval from Innocent IV in 1247. This is "the primitive rule" St. Teresa of Avila refers to as the original ideal of the order, to which she wished to return the order, even though unbeknownst to her it contained changes and mitigations approved by the Holy See. A century and a half later the struggle to maintain the contemplative ideal in the new circumstances of apostolic involvement led to the publication of The Book of the First Monks by the Catalonian provincial, Felip Ribot, in 1385. The book was a symbolic history of the order after the models of Elijah and Mary. It was like a directory of the spiritual life for the uprooted Carmelites, who looked wistfully to their origins on Mount Carmel.

Over the next two centuries the Carmelites underwent the vicissitudes of the times and struggled to be faithful to their calling, especially through a series of reforms in the 15th and 16th centuries that set the stage for the great Teresian or Discalced Reform under the leadership of St. Teresa of Avila (d.1582) and St. John of the Cross (d.1591). These gifted saints, who were later to be declared doctors of the church, put the stamp of greatness on the order and made Carmel synonymous with prayer. The Teresian Reform separated itself juridically from the Ancient Observance of the Carmelite Order in 1595 after the deaths of both saints. Discalced Carmel has distinguished itself over the last four hundred years in its number of canonized saints and teachers of prayer and the mystical life. Another reform, less celebrated but very significant for the order, was the Touraine Reform in 17th century France. It remained within the old Carmel and spread to all the provinces, accomplishing what Teresa of Jesus had hoped John of the Cross would do for the whole order.[2] The whole Carmelite family, both Discalced and Ancient Observance, men and women, religious and secular, first, second and third orders, live out of the rich tradition of Carmel and glory in the recent outstanding witnesses, such as the Little Flower, St. Therese of Lisieux (d.1896), St. Elizabeth of the Trinity (d. 1906), and the contemporary martyrs of the Holocaust, St. Edith Stein, O.C.D., and Blessed Titus Brandsma, O.Carm.

Our question now is this: how does Christian Meditation relate to the Carmelite tradition? This chapter gives a positive answer and shows how the new discipline can both enrich and be enriched by the Carmelite tradition of contemplative prayer.

An Historical Vignette

An interesting incident can set the stage for our inquiry. One of the first generation of Discalced Carmelite writers, José de J.-M Quiroga (1562-1628) set down the method of mental prayer taught by St. John of the Cross. It consisted of three steps: 1) the representation of some mysteries; 2) pondering them; and 3) experiencing the fruit of the process in "an attentive and loving quietude toward God," "a peaceful, loving and calm quiet of faith," or a "simple attention to God." [3] The method was obviously contemplative at least in the sense of contemplation in lectio divina. But it seems to be more categorical. The "loving quietude" and "simple attention" cited by Quiroga are the language of John of the Cross for contemplation. In John of the Cross what may be passing moments of contemplation become extended and coalesce into the habit or state of contemplation. Faithful practitioners of the meditation have acquired what John of the Cross calls the " spirit of meditation". They have sown many acts and reaped the habit of contemplation, or else in an alternative scenario, "God has placed them in [infused] contemplation without these means." St. John of the Cross sums up the outcome in what are described as two different graces, acquired and infused contemplation, concluding with these words:

What the soul was gradually acquiring through the labor of meditation on particular ideas has now been converted into habitual and substantial, general loving knowledge ... The moment it recollects itself in the presence of God it enters into the act of general, loving, peaceful, and tranquil knowledge, drinking wisdom, love and delight.[4]

According to Quiroga, John of the Cross expected his novices to reach at least this state of initial "acquired" contemplation by the end of the one-year novitiate, an opinion shared by Thomas of Jesus (1564-1627) and others.[5]

Christian Meditation is a different kind of meditation and is easily identified with the contemplative acts described by Quiroga. Meditators in this system are not told to expect a long preparatory phase, perhaps a year, before they will be graced with contemplation. The discrete acts of love start immediately and the habit or state of that condition will come later, either "acquired" through regular practice or "infused" by God's special grace. Either kind of contemplation is a valid outcome of meditation.[6] In John Main's perspective these distinctions are irrelevant. He leaves precise definitions to others and, as already indicated, he sees "contemplation, contemplative prayer, and meditative practice" as synonyms for meditation.[7] His meditation, moreover, is precisely the "loving quietude" and "simple attention" that marks the third stage of prayer described by Quiroga and taught by John of the Cross.

Today there is less concern about names and degrees of contemplation and more attention to the practice of contemplative disciplines. Thousands of devout Christians are pondering the mystery of God's presence in various forms of contemplative prayer.

They sit silently before an icon or the tabernacle and if asked they would describe their prayer as simple loving attention beyond words or images. Christian Meditation fits these perspectives. Its "contemplation" is not defined but includes all types of silent prayer, from quiet resting in the divine presence to infused contemplation.

The new style of contemplative prayer goes right to the heart of prayer, seeking experience and contact with the living God in loving faith and quiet presence. Christian Meditation is truly a "spiritual exercise," designed to elevate the whole spiritual life as aerobics or a workout in the gym tones up the physical body. The two periods of daily prayer are the anchors and the catalysts of the rest of the prayer life of the participant. These two periods represent a conversion, a commitment to a more serious prayer life. They are to be faithfully carried out as the first order of one's prayer life each day. The rest of one's spiritual life is energized from there. The discipline brings a contemplative dimension to the celebration of liturgy, to bible reading and the practice of lectio divina, to vocal prayer, to community life and ministry.

Christian Meditation is active prayer, but the activity is simple and receptive. One sits before the Lord, and the hoped-for outcome is the inbreaking of God "from the other side," the divine touch that is God's response to the human efforts, which themselves are antecedently inspired by God. The divine visit is validated only by the fruits of the Spirit. The person strives to be open and welcoming, to be empty and poor in spirit, and these attitudes are invitations to a deeper divine presence. Whatever the empirical experience in the human consciousness, the contemplative activity is bringing about transformation in the depths of the person, and this conversion will show itself in the person's life. The whole person - body, soul, and spirit - is engaged in the prayer. The body is brought into the process via posture, breathing, relaxation, and the use of a holy word or mantra. The psychological functions of understanding, willing and loving are definitely in play in muted, simple ways. The main task of the one praying is non-discursive attention.

The Carmelite Tradition

We are now ready to interface Christian Meditation and the Carmelite tradition. The latter will be represented in some key documents in its history, beginning with the earliest sources, The Rule of St. Albert and The Book of the First Monks, then the writings of Teresa of Avila and John of the Cross, and concluding with the Touraine Reform. The Rule describes a life rather than particular practices. So one popular artistic symbol, designed by the Dutch artist Arie Trum and entitled "No Image Satisfies," writes out the entire text by hand on a one-page script in cruciform shape with a golden circle in the center. The circle is dominant, and the entire copy of the Rule points to that center. The circle is at once empty and the place of encounter with God. The empty space represents "purity of heart", the condition for full "allegiance to Jesus Christ," a phrase in the prologue which sums up the vocation of the Carmelite. Emptiness and fullness are the core of the Carmelite rule.

The Rule itself is a collage of explicit and implicit citations from the bible. The word of God forms the Carmelite and it is mediated through the liturgy (daily Mass and the psalms originally read privately and later in the canonical hours), public bible reading at meetings and in the refectory, and above all through lectio divina prescribed in the famous Chapter 10: "Let all remain in their cells, or near them, meditating day and night on the law of the Lord and keeping vigil in prayer, unless occupied with other lawful duties." This is the defining chapter of the Rule, though the communitarian aspects are likewise foundational. The community is the place where personal transformation takes place and ministry originates. Solitude and community are opposite poles to be lived in creative tension.

What is the meaning of "meditating" and "keeping vigil in prayer" in this primary text of the Rule? The model will be the monastic practice of the time, which came from the Desert Fathers and Mothers through John Cassian and the ancient rules of Pachomius, Basil, and the Master. Monastic practice included many forms of praying, such as Our Father's, the psalms, the Jesus prayer, as well as different ways of reflecting on the word of God. One special way of meditating or pondering the word of God was repeating phrases of Scripture, often aloud. Cassian promotes this method and suggests the words, "O God, incline unto my aid: O Lord, make haste to help me." [8] This use of a mantra fits the prayer of the heart, which is Thomas Merton's "contemplative prayer," characterized as meditation in the Desert tradition.[9] This prayer is not intellectual analysis or active use of the imagination. Prayer of the heart consists in entering deeply into one's self to seek purity of heart, i.e. utter detachment and surrender to the indwelling God. The way to the heart is the word of God, biblical phrases repeated and pondered as in the Jesus prayer, which itself is a good example of the method in question. The goal is both transformation and continuous, loving conversation with God according to the exhortation of Chapters 18-19 of the Rule, which includes these words: "May you possess the sword of the spirit, which is God's word, abundantly in your mouth and in your hearts. Just so whatever you do, let it be done in the Lord's word."

This way of meditation was the "haga" tradition of the Old Testament, which consisted in reciting passages from Scripture aloud from memory, such as repeating short phrases of the psalms to root the words and sentiment in the mind and heart. The continuous repetition was called "murmuring," according to Kaes Waaijman, who writes that "one 'murmured' the Torah, 'ruminating' it until the text had completely become one's own, and began to 'sigh from within' as the cooing of a dove. One made the Torah his own bodily, emotionally, cognitively, memorizing it so that he ultimately became one with Torah." [10] The whole person was involved - the voice, the imagination, the feelings, the mind and heart - so that the whole person was to be "clothed" with the word of God. A new person emerged.

The method of meditating, therefore, was not objectified thinking, but pondering the word of God in one's heart, with one's whole interior being in non-discursive attention. Even the mouth and the tongue participated, so that the pondering was physical as well as interior. This was one reason for placing the solitary cells at a distance from each other in order not to disturb the neighbors by noisy prayer. The end in view, however, was both public praise and the transformation of the person, letting the word of God penetrate one's very being for a new, personal identity after the Scriptural model.

How close all this is to the mantra of John Main, the prayer of "selfless attention"? The Carmelite is called to the prayer of the heart, a prayer thoroughly contemplative in method and goal. The prayer is eminently simple and offers a direct route into the golden circle of Arie Trum, where self-emptying makes room for the living God.

The Book of the First Monks

The same perspectives of the Rule are found in The Book of the First Monks, the symbolic history of Elijah and spiritual directory for the Carmelites now living in new circumstances in Europe away from Mount Carmel. Originally the book purported to be history, then it was interpreted to be a record of myths and legends, and today it is regarded as a serious attempt to interpret Carmelite life through the life of Elijah and also of Mary, the Mother of Jesus. The mystical character of the Order is affirmed in the strongest terms with the same perspectives on emptiness and fullness found in the golden circle of Arie Trum.

The key passage is a commentary on the command to Elijah to "go eastward and hide in the brook Carith," where he would "drink of the torrent." (I Kings 17:2-4). The spiritual or mystical interpretation of these words is as follows:

The goal of this life is twofold. One part we acquire by our own effort and the exercise of the virtues, assisted by divine grace. This is to offer God a pure and holy heart, free from all stain of sin. We attain this goal when we are perfect and 'in Carith', that is, hidden in that love of which the Wiseman speaks: 'love covers all offenses'...

The other goal of this life is granted to us as the free gift of God, namely, to taste somewhat in the heart and to experience in the mind the power of the divine presence and the sweetness of heavenly glory, not only after death but already in this mortal life. This is to 'drink of the torrent' of the pleasure of God.[11]

In an unpublished paper delivered at a study week at the Washington Theological Union in September 1996, Hein Blommestijn used John Cassian to analyze this passage and to show that the twofold purpose is one movement of the Spirit with a proximate objective (skopos) and an ultimate goal (telos). The skopos is to present to God a pure heart; the telos to experience God. Like the farmer's planting and cultivating his field with a view to the harvest, the work of purification is engaged with the goal in sight of experiencing God. The first step occurs when one leaves one's own center and enters the empty circle; there God meets the person in a mystical encounter. The work is all God's. I enter the center and I become a new person, but both features are what God is doing in me. The self-emptying and the encounter continue progressively throughout life. They are one movement with two stages, not first a life of asceticism and then another of mysticism. "Before Elijah could take a single step," the Book says, "God had already set him in motion."[12]

The theology of Christian Meditation parallels this perspective of Felip Ribot expressed in the fourteenth century. The mantra is an exercise in self-emptying, the experience of poverty before God, and at the same time it is an invitation for God to come. John Cassian extends the role of the mantra beyond formal prayer into continuous prayer. The mantra thus becomes a way to practice the presence of God and mindfulness, the topic of the last chapter of this book. The following quotation underlines the fact that the mantra is a way of life and not just a technique. Cassian wrote:

> *You should, I say, meditate constantly on this verse in your heart. You should not stop repeating it when you are doing any kind of work or performing some service or are on a journey... This heart's reflection ...will purge you of every vice and earthly taint [and] lead you to the theoria [=contemplation] of invisible and heavenly realities and raise you to that ineffably ardent prayer which is experienced by very few.*[13]

The "ineffably ardent prayer" is "the prayer of fire," which is exalted contemplation, the same tasting of the divine presence promised by the *Book of the First Monks* as the outcome of "offering a pure heart to God." The *Book* and the *Conferences* of John Cassian on prayer are on the same page. One might even say that they are copies of each other as blueprints for living the Paschal Mystery.

St. Teresa of Avila

While Teresa had a prayer life before and after she entered Carmel in 1535, she confesses that she did not know how to go about praying until 1538, three years after she entered the order, when she discovered Francis of Osuna's Third Spiritual Alphabet. (Book of Her Life 4.7) There she learned in a new way the fact of the divine Indwelling and prayer as contact with the living God. "We need no wings to go in search of him," she wrote, "but have only to find a place where we can be alone and look upon him present within us." (The Way of Perfection 28.2)

Temperamentally Teresa could not search in discursive prayer, nor could she control her restless imagination and memory. Methodical meditation was an impossibility for her. She wrote for people like herself, "for souls and minds so scattered that they are like wild horses no one can stop." (The Way of Perfection 19.2) Prayer for her was presence, loving presence, a fact she learned from Osuna as the heart of "recollection." Recollection was gathering up one's soul, "collecting all one's faculties together and entering within itself to be with its God." (The Way of Perfection 28.4) Thus one moves within beyond the confining world of creatures into the sacred space of God.

Active recollection is the person's own doing. Once recollected one fruitfully practices vocal prayer like the Our Father. Recollection and vocal prayer were Teresa's mainstay. With gaze fixed on Christ she prayed the Our Father; this double practice was her recommendation for everyone and an easy way to the prayer of quiet. (The Way of Perfection 28.4) [14]

Teresa also practiced and taught a silent prayer of recollection that is the counterpart of Christian Meditation but without the mantra. If the mantra is the prayer of Christian Meditation, as John Main avers, how can active recollection be the counterpart? The reason is the internal dynamics are the same in both prayers: the non-discursive attention and making one's self vulnerable to the transforming power of God. Teresa does not invoke a holy word at all; instead she uses an image from the Passion of Jesus to refocus when necessary.

Her method of active recollection is as follows. First, she strove to be present to Christ within. She used many stratagems to find this recollection, such as a book at hand like a Linus blanket to be utilized as needed, inviting favorite saints like Mary Magdalene and the Samaritan woman to accompany her, holy cards, nature scenes. But her main strategy and the very goal of the prayer was "representing Christ interiorly." (Book of Her Life 4.7; The Way of Perfection 28.4)

The phrase is peculiarly Teresian. It does not mean imagining Christ – Teresa had no ability to use her imagination. "Representing Christ interiorly" means realizing that Christ is present now in her soul. "Realizing" means to make real, and the outcome is real knowledge as compared with notional knowledge in the famous distinction of Cardinal Newman. Real knowledge is holistic, the product of all the faculties working together. It uncovers the real presence of the living Christ, really present both objectively and subjectively. He is there; "your Spouse never takes his eyes off you." (The Way of Perfection 26.3) She does not see him; but he is there as if in the darkness, and he can be apprehended the way a blind person recognizes another person in the room. Representing Christ for Teresa means tuning into that real presence.

But, you say, does not Teresa counsel imagining Christ in some mystery of the Passion? Yes, she recommends recalling Christ suffering in Gethsemane or at the pillar when awareness and attention are fading. The recalls are accessory, quick images to reinvigorate a fading loving attention. They are only subsidiary means to heighten the sense of presence. The images are super-imposed on the reality of the Christ within and put a face on the faceless Christ. The essence of the prayer is not the image, but the realization of the divine presence. The image comes and goes as needed to refocus.

This method soon brought Teresa into mystical experiences of quiet and union. Notice how she connects these graces with the practice of "representing Christ":

> *It used to happen, when I represented Christ within me in order to place myself in His presence, or even while reading, that a feeling of the presence of God would come over me unexpectedly so that I could in no way doubt He was in me or I totally immersed in Him. This did not occur after the manner of a vision. I believe they call the experience "mystical theology." (Book of Her Life 10.1)*

Her full entry into the mystical state came after a long, subsequent struggle of l8 to 20 years. It took that long to integrate her whole being in God. Throughout this period as well as afterwards her basic strategy at prayer was the prayer of active recollection twice daily for an hour each time. This was one of the foundations of her reform. Today Christian Meditation recommends two briefer periods of the prayer with the same ultimate goal of personal reform and renewal. Teresa's active recollection is essentially the same means to sanctity as Christian Meditation.

St. John of the Cross

John of the Cross does not describe an equivalent of Teresa's active recollection in his writings. He has only two ways of relating to God, which he calls "meditation" and "contemplation". Meditation for him describes self-directed activity and contemplation pure receptivity before God. They are adequately distinct from one another. This 'discursive meditation' utilizes our faculties and human potential to come to know and love God, always under grace. 'Contemplation' is infused light and love that are the pure gifts of God. The word contemplation in both Teresa of Avila and John of the Cross is always the infused gift. John calls meditation a natural operation, contemplation a supernatural one; this terminology is peculiar to Teresa, John, and others of the time.

We saw in the first part of this paper that early followers of John developed a theory of "acquired contemplation" and appealed to his authority for the teaching. For some interpreters acquired contemplation is an oxymoron, a contradiction in terms. For others the achievement of the habit or state of quiet, loving, restful presence to God beyond words and images as the result of faithful practice of interior prayer is a real possibility. Acquired contemplation does not go beyond beginning contemplation, the experience described by John as "loving awareness of God, without particular considerations, in interior peace and quiet and repose, and without the acts and exercises (at least discursive, those in which one progresses from point to point)...." (Ascent 2.13.4) This "general, loving awareness" lacks the specific difference that defines infused contemplation for many theologians, namely, the mystical union of felt experience of God. Acquired contemplation is "ordinary" contemplation in contrast to the extraordinary contemplation of mystical union. It is a possible outcome of active contemplative practice.

Christian Meditation is definitely "active" contemplative practice. The loving attention it espouses comes from one's own initiative and deliberate choice and is different from the pure receptivity in infused contemplation, which John describes as the awareness of "a person who opens his eyes with loving attention." (Living Flame of Love 3.33) The person opens her eyes and light and love pour from God into the soul. She is "doing nothing" in the strongest sense of that phrase. Active contemplative practice is doing something and this is why this practice belongs to meditation in John of the Cross's schema.

At first sight John of the Cross may not seem to speak as directly to budding contemplatives as Teresa, but in fact his teaching zeroes in on the essentials. He spells out in his extended treatment of the active and passive purifications what The Rule of St. Albert and The Book of the First Monks set down in global terms. The two early documents of the order and Teresa of Avila and John of the Cross are all translating the Paschal Mystery of death and resurrection into practical directives.

Death and resurrection are achieved in the contemplative through the practice of loving faith. Faith is the only proximate means of union with God, says John of the Cross, and this principle applies to the whole journey. Why is this so? Because faith screens out all that is not of God and welcomes God in all God's truth and beauty. Our Blessed Lady is the perfect example of this principle. She is the woman of faith, who listens and carries out the word of God. She is a window without spot, through which the sunlight passes through without hindrance and so envelopes her that it is impossible to tell where the sunlight ends and the window begins. All her choices come from faith; she waits on the word of God and follows it completely. There are no other options in her life. God dominates everything. God and her soul (herself) are "one in participant transformation, and the soul appears to be God more than a soul." (Ascent 2.5.7) This is the same one goal of all contemplative prayer.

Touraine Reform

The Touraine Reform is the glory of the Ancient Observance of the Carmelite Order. The reform began in the French province of Touraine in 1608 under the leadership of Philip Thibault (1572-1638); it spread through the lowlands and eventually to the whole Order. The most famous spiritual leader in the reform was the blind brother, John of St. Samson, who has been called the French John of the Cross. The old Order lives by the spirit of Touraine more than any other influence.

Like the Teresian forerunner Touraine was not just aggiornamento or upgrading monastic discipline. It was a return to the primitive spirit of the Order, which Kilian Healy describes as "a life that was primarily (but not exclusively) contemplative wherein the spirit of solitude, silence and prayer reign supreme." [15] To this end the reform produced a significant body of spiritual literature, one element of which were four volumes of directories for novices. The fourth volume, whose Latin short title is Methodus orandi, treats discursive meditation, affective prayer, the prayer of simple regard (equated with acquired contemplation) as forms of active prayer that dispose the subject for infused contemplation. This is traditional teaching. What is special in the Methodus is aspirative prayer or aspirations, which is treated as part of the illuminative way and a direct means to the unitive way of mystical union. It is a favorite topic in Touraine, because aspirative prayer is seen as the way to fulfill Chapter 10 of the Rule on continuous, loving conversation with God, which for Touraine is the very purpose of the Order.

Aspirative prayer is a step or two beyond ejaculatory prayer; it is more intense, more fervent, and it comes from a purified heart. Aspirations are not just any holy thoughts or desires or even affectionate conversation. They are "darts out of the flaming fire of love," and as such beyond the ability of beginners and possible only for people who love God deeply and authentically and are on the way to mystical union. In the view of Touraine "the most simple affection is worth more than all the thoughts that are written in books," [16] and aspirations are special affections in which "all the affections of the heart are in the one word." [17]

The Methodus considers aspiratory prayer as coming after and building on previous discursive and affective prayer. This way of praying belongs in the same level as Christian Meditation and all explicit forms of contemplative prayer. Its place in the life of the spirit is more flexible now than it was in the late Middle Ages. Like everything associated with contemplation in the 17th century, aspiratory prayer was considered to be a higher form of prayer. Were Christian Meditation to have existed at that time, it would have been restricted to souls in the illuminative way. In Touraine, as in the rest of the Catholic world at the time, the four acts of lectio divina had become stages of prayer rather than parts of one organic whole. There were four degrees: vocal prayer, discursive meditation, affective prayer and finally contemplation, and the last of the series was either active and acquired, or else passive and infused contemplation. The three forms of mental (i.e. non-vocal) prayer corresponded to the three stages of spiritual development, namely, the purgative, illuminative, and unitive ways. Practitioners were locked into the prayer form that belonged to their stage. The words of one great master of the period, Louis Lallemant, were typical: "Everyone should remain faithful to the prayer proper to the degree or state of his (sic) spiritual life." [18]

Contemporary thinking breaks out of these hard and fast categories. No doubt some previous experience in mental prayer is helpful or even necessary for contemplative practice, but prayer is not quantified, and we pray the way God gives us to pray. Rigidity and inflexibility serve no purpose. Yet the teaching of the past has its own wisdom. If Guiges II thought that the four acts were so interconnected that they were always to be performed in sequence, so that "it would be a rare exception or a miracle to gain contemplation without prayer," [19] then it behooves us to make room for prayer, oratio, before contemplation itself. Christian Meditation can well fit in between the third and the fourth acts of lectio divina, which are prayer and contemplation. It is both prayer and contemplation structured together.

Aspirative prayer has not been developed into a distinct method or discipline like Christian Meditation. But it can easily be integrated into the current practice of Christian Meditation by letting it reinforce the love that is the essence of all contemplative prayer. The addition of aspirative prayer highlights something already there and it can serve to put the emphasis where it belongs, namely, on the primordial role of love. The aspirative prayer tradition can enrich Christian Meditation, a view which is treated at length in chapter seven of this book.

Conclusion

What conclusions can we draw from this brief inquiry? It is clear that the Carmelite tradition and Christian Meditation dovetail. They fit beautifully together. Christian Meditation is a concrete way of carrying out Chapter 10 of the Rule and incarnates its overall meaning as interpreted by Arie Trum. Christian Meditation is an enfleshment of the orientation of the Carmelite Order as described in The Book of the First Monks, in which the immediate task is presenting a pure heart to God and the ultimate goal as experiencing the divine presence. The double purpose is the Carmelite way of living the

Paschal Mystery. The monastic prayer of the heart in Chapter 10 of The Rule of St. Albert is like a foreshadowing of Christian Meditation. The prayer of active recollection of St. Teresa of Avila highlights the rationale and the underlying principles of Christian Meditation. Teresa did not employ the mantra, but she suggested her own ways of maintaining selfless attention and non-discursive presence. Essentially the two ways of praying are the same. The method of mental prayer attributed to John of the Cross by Quiroga is close to Christian Meditation in its goal of contemplative presence and the downplaying of rational, discursive meditation in favor of pondering. Christian Meditation receives validation and enlightenment from the teaching of John of the Cross as well as the Touraine doctrine of aspirations.

In theory and in practice Christian Meditation offers new ways of understanding and applying the Carmelite tradition. In other words Christian Meditation is not only compatible, it proceeds from the same basic philosophy and theology as the Carmelite tradition and as such can be an update and an appealing way of fulfilling the Carmelite vocation. John Main and the teachers of this new discipline breathe the same air and work out of similar understandings of what the Christian life of prayer should be. The old tradition of Carmel congratulates and thanks the World Community for Christian Meditation for the new things and old that it draws from the rich storehouse of the western mystical tradition.

Endnotes

1 *John Cassian: the Conferences* (tr. Boniface Hanley, O.P., New York: Paulist Press, 1997) and *John Cassian: the Institutes* Boniface Hanley,O.P., New York: Newman Press, 2000)

2 Foundations 3.17.

3 The testimony of Quiroga and the phrases in quotation marks are recorded by James Arraj, *From John of the Cross to Us* (Chiloquin, OR: Inner Growth Books, 1999) 103-104. In this book James Arraj reopens the question of John of the Cross' teaching and acquired contemplation. He denies that John taught acquired contemplation and accuses followers of misinterpreting the master. Arraj lays blame for the Quietist errors of the 17th century and the malaise about mysticism in the 18th and 19th centuries on what he considers to be this false teaching about acquired contemplation. The present article takes an opposite view and sees acquired contemplation as a legitimate concept.

4 The quotations in this paragraph are from the *Ascent of Mt. Carmel 2.14.2*

5 Arraj, *ibid*, 64-65

6 The controversy about acquired contemplation is largely laid to rest today in favor of seeing acquired contemplation and initial infused contemplation as basically the same experience with different theological explanations. Authors avoid the distinction today. For a classical defense of acquired contemplation see Gabriel of St. Mary Magdalen, O.C.D., *St John of the Cross, Doctor of Divine Love,* which contains the separate entry of *Acquired Contemplation* (pp.100-202)(Westminster, Md: Newman, 1946). For an attempt to offer an irenic interpretation of the terminology of contemplation, see my essay, "Contemporary Prayer Forms – Are they Contemplation?" *Review for Religious* 57 (1998) 77-87.

7 *Talks on Meditation* (Montreal:1979) 10.

8 *The Conferences, Tenth Conference on Prayer* 10.2. Simon Tugwell points out that Guigo II, one of the earliest architects of *lectio divina*, equated meditating with repeating the word. See his *Ways of Imperfection* (Springfield: Templegate, 1985) 94-95;105.

9 William H.Shannon, *Thomas Merton's Paradise Journey* (Cincinnati:St Anthony, 2000) 188-205.

10 *The Mystical Space of Carmel* (Amsterdam: Peeters, 1999

11 Felip Ribot,O.Carm., *The Ten Books on the Way of Life and Great Deeds of the Carmelites,* [including] *The Book of the First Monks* (ed and tr Richard Copsey, O.Carm.,Roma: Edizioni Carmelitane, 2005) bk I, ch 2, p.9

12 *Ibid, 5,*

13 *Tenth Conference* 10.14.

14 Kieran Kavanaugh, O.C.D., "Introduction" to the *Interior Castle* (New York:Paulist Press) 12-15

15 *Methods of Prayer in the Directory of the Carmelite Reform of Touraine* (Rome:Institutum Carmelitanum, 1956)16.

16 *Methodus*, cited in Healy, 63.

17 John Brenninger, O.Carm., *The Carmelite Directory of the Spiritual Life* (tr. Leo J. Walter, O.Carm., Chicago: Carmelite Press, l951) 471.

18 Cited in Paul Philippe, O.P. "Mental Prayer in the Catholic Tradition," in *Mental Prayer and Modern Life, a Symposium* (tr. Francis C. Lehner, New York: Kennedy, l950) 3.

19 *Scala claustralium*, cited in Philippe, 23.

Chapter Five

Christian Meditation and Desert Spirituality

The desert is a rich metaphor for several aspects of spirituality, all of which relate to Christian Meditation and provide a healthy support for its practice. The physical desert in Scripture is primarily a wasteland like large areas of Egypt and the Middle East, but it comes alive in verdant splendor on luxuriant mountain slopes or the gardens of the promised land. Thus Isaiah writes: "The desert shall rejoice and blossom... The glory of Lebanon shall be given it, the majesty of Carmel and Sharon." (35:1-2) The desert has both negative and positive symbolism.

It is, first of all, a place of struggle, where conversion and purification take place, where wrestling with a hostile environment is symbolic of the fight for self-mastery and victory over demons. But it is also the place for rich positive experiences, such as the encounter with God in the burning bush for Moses on Mt. Sinai (Ex 3:2) or in "a sound of sheer silence," sometimes identified as a gentle breeze, at the cave on Mt Horeb for Elijah. (1 Kings 19:12)

The desert is a place of personal renewal and refreshment, and not only spiritually, but physically and emotionally as well. The human quality of life is enhanced by a day in the desert. At the same time the desert presents an immense ecological challenge and cries out for the concern and help of human beings. Its pristine and fragile beauty needs the oversight and cooperation of people, if it is to survive into the future. The desert is a threatened environment, and it should be high on the social agenda of the people of God.

The primary concern of desert spirituality is the spiritual one of self-discovery and encounter with God. The desert envisioned is a symbolic one, and not necessarily the geographical place that goes by this name. It is any place of solitude and silence, such as attic room or open countryside, where the deep issues of life can be faced. This is the spiritual desert. It remains true, however, that the spiritual desert thrives best in the actual desert. All the aspects mentioned so far are part of "desert spirituality" and will be addressed in this chapter.

First we look at the spiritual meaning of the desert as a metaphor for purification and encounter with God. Then we will look at the invitation and offering of the physical desert as a place for pursuing true leisure and recreation. Finally we will examine the environmental issue of proper stewardship of the desert.

Desert Spirituality in History

Desert spirituality originates in the bible, in both the Hebrew and Christian Scriptures. It was lived experience for the Israelites at the time of the Exodus, and it became a way of life for some early Christian elites, who developed an eremetical and monastic life style in the deserts of Egypt and the Middle East. These people were the Desert Fathers and Mothers, the *abbas* and the *ammas* of the third, fourth and fifth centuries of the Christian era.

Some familiar biblical experiences of the desert are the forty-year wandering of Israel in the Exodus story, the heroics in the life of Elijah both on the wooded slopes of Mt. Carmel and across the sands of the Judean desert, the call to Hosea to go out to the desert to be espoused to God, the ministry of John the Baptist, the forty-day fast of Jesus in the wilderness, and the novitiate of Paul in Arabia. (Gal 1:17) These incidents illustrate the harshness and the grace of the desert.

The Desert Fathers and Mothers fled to the wilderness to escape the decadence of an effete Roman empire. The wasteland offered a stark and untrammeled setting for a life of penance and prayer. Its rugged emptiness and its silence and solitude invited *fuga mundi,* flight from the world. A special appeal was the belief that the demons infested the wilderness and could be met there for open combat. It did not take long for the desert dwellers to discover that the demons were within and to be engaged on the battleground of the soul.

John Cassian has preserved the traditions of these early Christian attempts at monastic living, and Christian Meditation is part of this patrimony. Christian Meditation does not come from Cassian as a finished product, but it finds its philosophical roots there. The mantra is found as the repetition of a particular phrase from Scripture and is presented as a legitimate and effective way of praying for Christians. The mantra is not an exclusive property of the East, of the Hindus, for example, from whom John Main originally learned its use of a mantra style. Cassian validated the use of the mantra in John Main's prayer. The classic name for the repetition of one word or phrase prayer is "monologistic prayer," or "one-word prayer." John Main constructed his own version of monologistic prayer and put the method back in practice for thousands of meditators.[1] A more important contribution from John Cassian is the theoretical foundations of meditative prayer, such as the goal of continuous prayer, the stages of prayer that culminate in "the prayer of fire" or exalted contemplation, and the dynamics of cultivating purity of heart in order to "see" God, which are the *skopos* and *telos* of monastic life. Purity of heart or poverty of spirit is directly cultivated by the genius of the mantra because of the impoverishment it fosters. The mantra is the instrument of purity of heart. For this reason Christian Meditation is a way of life, a discipline that goes to the heart of the Christian life. It is not just a particular method of praying.

The whole daily life of the hermits and monks contributed to their purification and enlightenment. It is so for Christian Meditators as well, whose daily tasks in their own different vocations provide the opportunities for daily asceticism.

Life in the desert was more simple than most people's lives today. Manual labor broke the monotony of the silence and solitude and provided its own asceticism as well as sustenance and a source for almsgiving. Desert dwellers spent their days in soul-searching and the pursuit of the living God. Community life, especially when the solitary life prevailed, and outreach in ministry were clearly not a major part of the desert lifestyle. Continuous prayer was the goal and the *abbas* and the *ammas* spent their time in *lectio divina*, reading the psalms, celebrating liturgy, and cultivating the prayer of the heart. Their ultimate aim was to reach "the prayer of fire," the summit of prayer which left the person uplifted and inflamed with the love of God and in this way accomplishing the goal of continuous prayer.[2]

In this setting striving for Christian holiness was a white martyrdom, a total giving over of one's life to God. Life in the desert was a studied effort to shed self-indulgence and live out a single-minded search for God. The desert was a graphic reminder of the emptiness of life and the otherness of God. The emptiness translated into purity of heart, a heart seeking only God's will and freedom from sinful affections. This was simply the application of the guiding principle of desert spirituality and the way of the beatitude, "Blessed are the pure of heart, for they shall see God." (Mt 5:8)

This beatitude is the rock-bottom foundation of all monastic living. It applies to all Christian vocations, since everyone must let go of earth-bounded concerns in order to participate fully in the holiness or otherness of God. The dyad of the beatitude is the explicit framework for the heart of desert spirituality. The physical desert remains the place of choice for the few hardy souls, but the symbolic desert is a challenge to every serious Christian.

Anthony and Pachomius spurned the fleshpots of the Roman cities and went to the bleak solitude of Egypt as spiritual athletes, to be alone with God and to keep careful watch over the movements of their hearts. The purity of heart they sought was total. They tried to recognize and resist the first movements of any thought or desire that threatened their purity of heart. Their single purpose was to put to death the old man within themselves and promote the new life that was God's gift. They underwent this discipline for one reason: they wanted to see God. This goal was not face to face vision, as we believe heaven will be (1 John 3:1-3); nor was it seeing God as an object, the way I see a person in front of me; God is not an object, but infinite spirit. The seeing is not just a new understanding, a new image of God, or a new perception. It is contemplative union with God, knowing God in the way I know myself; it is walking with God as a loving companion. God is as real to the person as the person is to herself. God and self are co-known in the ineffable dance of life. There is the oneness of experience, a oneness in mystery that evaporates the moment one tries to seize it, objectify it or explain it. It is simply there. It is life and experience, communion in being beyond expression. And the bottom line is that such participation in God's life is as deep and intense as one's purity of heart.

There are many ways of expressing the concept of purity of heart. It is freedom from actual sin; it is having right relationships with self, others, the world, and God. Purity of heart is more than the virtue of chastity; it is all the virtues in perfect harmony and integration. This marvelous condition often uses negative terminology, such as detachment, or indifference, or freedom from sin. Actually it is a very positive condition, which finds clear expression in the phrase, biblical faith. All the different terms are synonyms for biblical faith. This faith is the response to the word of God wherever it is recognized. It is the faith of the Virgin Mary in St. Luke's gospel. At the annunciation, for example, she is perturbed at the angel Gabriel's message. How can she, a committed virgin, be the mother of the Messiah? When the angel assures her that God will provide, she gives her full assent to that word. She lets go of her own project in favor of God's word. That is biblical faith.

A high degree of purity of heart means a heart full of faith and love. The pure of heart are loving persons. They will see God, i.e. they will know and love God as the indwelling God within themselves, in their brothers and sisters, and in all creation, as John writes in his first letter: "Beloved, let us love one another, because love is from God; everyone who loves is born of God and knows God. Whoever does not love does not know God, for God is love... No one has ever seen God; if we love one another, God lives in us, and his love is perfected in us." (I John 4:7-8,12)

Seeing God for the Desert Fathers and Mothers and especially for theologians like Evagrius of Pontus meant contemplation. This gift was the reward for the taxing work of purification. The precise nature of contemplation is difficult to describe: it is an incommunicable subjective state. It is the presence and experience of union with God. This is not any one particular, psychological experience, nor even new objective knowledge. It is not an altered state of consciousness. It is the fact of transformation and communion or oneness of being with God. By allowing one's life to be brought under the movement of the Holy Spirit, a new person is born. The person is a "new creation" (2 Cor 5:17), who lives in the world of God and experiences God in the whole gamut of his or her worldly occupations in the same way we experience ourselves in those actions. In other words it has many faces, all of them beyond recounting. Contemplation happens wherever the contemplative lives and acts, in work and play as well as prayer.

A Carmelite Application

We have already seen in the last chapter that the ideal of purity of heart and contemplation were the self-description of Carmelite life in the 14th century. The Carmelite Order was born on Mount Carmel, which was less a desert than a verdant mountain range in northern Israel overlooking the Mediterranean Sea. Mount Carmel was home to the prophet Elijah, to Elisha his successor, and to the guild of prophets that continued afterwards. Some two millennia later, in the early 13th century, in an area on Mount Carmel called the Wadi-es-en Siah, a small group of hermits came together to establish their own community. They petitioned the Latin patriarch for a manifesto, a "formula of life," which they could follow in imitation of Elijah, their model and ideal. They were as well devoted to the Blessed Mother and had built an oratory in her name.

The times were turbulent, with ongoing hostility between the Crusaders and the Muslims, both of whom were struggling to control the region. The Crusaders had succeeded in liberating the Holy Land, but victory was tenuous and faded away in the disastrous battle of Hattin in 1187. The Europeans lost control of all but a slender piece of land along the coast from Tyre to Jaffa. The hermits of Carmel trace their origins to this period and they were organized into a community in the time of the Latin patriarch, Albert Avogadro, in the early twelve hundreds. By 1238 they were forced to vacate their holy ground and begin to seek refuge in Europe. Their purely eremitical life style did not fare well in Europe and gradually they accommodated to the dominant form of religious life at the time, which was that of mendicant friars like the Dominicans and Franciscans. The simple lifestyle on Mount Carmel had to give way to coenobitic community and an active, apostolic ministry. The eremetical and contemplative spirit remained their true spirit, but it could be lived in its pure form only by way of exception. The Carmelites were busy about many things after the example of their mendicant brothers. This was the context of *The Institution of the First Monks.*

One of the priors general, Nicholas the Frenchman, tried to stem the tide and wrote a strong letter, called "The Fiery Arrow," dated 1270, calling the men to return to the desert. But the mendicant form of life, which they had gradually assumed with papal approval, had become a political and economic necessity as well as the choice of the men. To be friars living in the midst of the people had struck a chord in their hearts, and they embraced the reconstruction of their Carmelite vocation. Henceforth the Carmelites would have to carry the desert in their hearts, as most active Christians have to do.

The prophet Elijah and the Blessed Virgin Mary were still the models of the new desert life.

The life of Elijah became the description and defense of the new lifestyle. Felip Ribot's book incorporated a great deal of John Cassian as an interpretive key for the biblical account of Elijah. The result in Ribot was a desert spirituality that would be lived out in the towns and cities. Carmelites adapted the high ideals of the true First Monks, the Desert Fathers and Mothers, to the active life. There would always be room for those who wanted to go out into the physical desert. But the majority would live an apostolic life. The struggle for all Carmelites, religious and lay alike, then and now, was to be faithful to the eremetical and contemplative ideal. *The Book of the First Monks* was their charter, second in importance only to the *Rule of St. Albert.* The *Book* was the blueprint of the great reforms in the order's history, including the Discalced Reform of St. Teresa of Avila and St. John of the Cross. These great doctors of the church brought the eremetical-contemplative ideal to perfection. They did so, not only by promoting desert houses of total contemplative life, but by organizing and directing that every Carmelite house would be, in the words of another great Carmelite of the next century, John of St. Samson, another Mount Carmel.

Other Aspects of Desert Spirituality

We have discussed the meaning of the spiritual desert in terms of its foundational principles, which are the primordial role of purity of heart and its crowning reward of contemplation. These principles are the goals of Christian Meditation. But there is more to desert spirituality than these two principles. The physical desert invites engagement on the level of human development and challenges the concerned to care for it and preserve it for future generations. These two issues are not directly part of the mission of Christian Meditation, but as integral parts of a well-rounded spiritual life, they deserve a place in the lives of Christian Meditators. A full Christian life pursues wellness and wholeness in one's self and healthy concern for larger social issues like ecology and the environment. These dimensions can truly be part of the agenda for those who choose to follow the path of Christian Meditation.

Each of the two issues can be put in the form of a question. The first question is this: what can the desert do for me? The second is, what can I do for the desert? Both questions are part of an incarnational spirituality, which is concerned about the temporal world as well as the eternal one. We move from the transcendent to immanent considerations, from fleeing the world to embracing it.

The *via negativa* is the way of skirting the goods of creation in order to fasten on God, and the *via positiv* uses the goods of creation to move toward God. The present questions belong to the *via positiva.* They pertain to creation spirituality. Growth in personal wholeness and safeguarding the earth are typical concerns in this perspective. How can we use creation to develop our own and others' human potential as a ladder to God? How can we engage to the fullest the beautiful gift of the pristine desert in our journey to God? These questions apply to those who love this world and they should be concerns for Christian Meditators, who are called to union with God but with their feet firmly planted on the ground where they stand.

What Can the Desert Do for Me?

Why should I go out into the desert? The desert is barren sand dunes and the scrubby flat lands as well as verdant gardens, scenic forests, majestic mountains and rolling plains, national parks and forest preserves. The desert is all the places on this beautiful earth that are still largely untouched by city sprawl. They offer themselves as a refuge for weary citizens. These lands can be gift for our spirits. They refresh us and challenge us. They beckon us to "come aside and rest a while," away from the noise and congestion of the city, its polluted air and harried traffic. The desert is the place to hike a trail, fish a stream, picnic with friends, or just smell the roses and be with one's long thoughts.

Except for the few hermits in our midst most people only visit the desert; they do not live there. They go there for physical exercise and emotional refreshment, for meditation and for fun. They enter the desert places that are hostile to human habitation gingerly, armed with water jug, proper sun gear and ideally with companions. Some visit these "fierce landscapes", a phrase coined by author Belden Lane, for excitement, others to deal with a crisis, face a limit experience, or sit with a sorrow that overwhelms them. Perhaps unconsciously they are looking for an environment that mirrors their troubled soul. A good example of this kind of match-up between soul and terrain is a retreat for middle-aged men reported in a recent Irish journal.[3] The retreat was designed to help the men through their mid-life crisis. The retreat took place at Ghost Ranch in northern New Mexico in the summer of 2000. The men were challenged to let down their defenses and face themselves squarely. The retreat turned out to be a harrowing rite of passage. The torrid summer heat and the lonely emptiness of the desert combined with soul searching rituals and introspection to test the most stouthearted.

More often retreats or "a day in the desert" are spent in more friendly spaces. An attractive pastoral setting calms the soul and gives the quiet needed for looking at the real issues of one's life. God seems closer in virgin settings. One popular formula for such outings is the "poustinia", a concept popularized by Catherine de Hueck. Poustinia means hermitage, and participants become "poustiniks" for a day, bringing along only a bible and a bit of bread and cheese. The poustinia can actually be a back room or the attic of one's home, but there are advantages in going out to the woods or the seashore.

Getting out into the country, breathing in the fresh air and fragrances of the meadows, walking around the lake or trudging along paths in hilly terrain can be healthy, physical exercise and spiritual refreshment. These walks offer ways of slowing down, of refusing to be a couch potato and insuring the balance of "mens sana in corpore sano " (a sound mind in a sound body). Grace builds on nature, so a healthy body and soul are a good substructure for the life of God in us, particularly for a serious prayer life. A good health regime works directly against anxious, workaholic tendencies or the equally bad habit of inertia and laziness. Recreational activities also develop the playful side of our lives. This is our contemplative side.

Visitors to the desert know that God is everywhere and that they don't have to go up to the heavens or across the sea to find God. "No," Deuteronomy says, "the word is very near to you; it is in your mouth and in your heart for you to observe." (Deut 30:11-14) But the desert facilitates the search. The wide open spaces, the silence and solitude reveal God. Silence is the best contact point with God, since God is always present and exists beyond speech, images and concepts. The desert fosters silence, emptiness, and letting go of everything that is not of God. The desert is built for *kenosis,* the self-emptying of Jesus, who was perfectly open to God and was therefore exalted with the *pleroma,* the fullness of the Resurrection. (Phil 2:5 -11) The desert way is the way of emptiness and fullness.

These reflections are elementary and belong to the first steps in the spiritual journey. The appreciation of creation is the recognition of the original blessing, which precedes original sin, and immersion in creation and appreciation and love for this gift ought to precede the work of purification. This is the thinking of Teilhard de Chardin, Matthew Fox, Francis Kelly Nemeck, Maria Coombs and many others. More recently Dorothee Soelle sees "being amazed" as the first of the three ways or stages of the spiritual life. Instead of the classical ways of purification, illumination and union, she proposes "being amazed, letting go, and resisting" as the three steps. Amazement and appreciation help us take an objective stance before the earth, and this makes it easier to let go, the second of the three ways for Soelle. This leads us to involvement, to compassion and commitment regarding the world's needs. She calls this resistance, because it involves working against lines of least resistance in the environment and society. Resistance belongs to work for justice in all areas of life, such as the economic and the ecological orders.[4] This brings us to the second question regarding our relationship to the natural world about us.

What Can I Do for the Desert?

The second question is a prophetic one: what can I do for the desert? Uninhabited lands, especially when they are attractive or otherwise inviting, are often under attack by the forces of neglect or consumerism. How does my involvement in protecting the environment or my failure to do so impact my own personal life?

Participation in the work of saving the earth can be an important element in our own spiritual growth. Such involvement commits one to a worthy cause, one that offers something to the world. The new cosmology presented by scientists like Brian Swimme and the "geologian," Thomas Berry C.P, as well as the constant refrain from environmentalists that the earth is wounded and in danger of destruction sound an alarm that must be answered by responsible people. The universe and *homo sapiens* are one vast living organism that depends on both parties and will rise and fall with each other.

In the past the earth was looked upon as an appendage of humanity. Humanity alone counted and the rest of creation was expendable. Human beings pursued their own desires recklessly without thought about the effects on the environment. They could trash the earth, abuse it or destroy it by over-consumption without worry, because there were always other virgin territories to exploit in the same way. This was an affront to creation; it is also an affront to human life as well, because in the words of Edward Abbey, "the wilderness is not a luxury but a necessity of the human spirit just as vital to our lives as water and good bread."[5] The universe is an integral part of our human life; we are partners together and we participate in mutual growth or decline. In the abuse or destruction of the universe we are diminished and dehumanized. In protecting and enhancing the natural world we are enriched.

The commission in Genesis 1:26 for human beings to have "dominion" over the earth did not give them the right to abuse it. We are only caretakers, not absolute owners; all too easily people take the myopic view of seeing only the immediate return in pleasure or profit with no concern for the long term loss and the short-changing of fellow human beings in the bargain. One reviewer of Thomas Berry's latest book, *The Great Work, Our Way into the Future,* quotes a passage from Berry and then adds these strong words:

> *"What happens to the outer world happens to the inner world," Berry avers. "If the outer world is diminished in its grandeur then the emotional, imaginative, intellectual, and spiritual life of the human is diminished or extinguished." Our inner being will die if we continue to transform natural beauty into the soul-deadening, concrete-laden, box-store landscapes of a consumer society.*[6]

The obligation to safeguard the environment has three aspects: personal, societal, and spiritual. Each person needs to treat the desert with love and respect. Some of that concern is cosmetic like cleaning up after using the land and properly disposing of the debris, especially non-biodegradable material. Respect and moderation mean that we do not harm the plant life by careless trampling, that we obey rules about camp fires and camping, that we leave the natural beauty intact without pilfering plants or otherwise harming the vegetation, that we introduce no toxic substances like pesticides or poisonous chemicals. These are common sense suggestions.

The societal obligation may take the form of supporting societies like the Sierra Club that are dedicated to the environment, or to lend one's name to movements like Robert Redford's campaign to save the Arctic wilderness. The big problems can be addressed only by legislation and concerted group efforts. We need to support these causes. There is no other way to stop the pollution of our waterways and atmosphere, to keep industrial wastes out of our rivers and lakes, to find adequate ways of dealing with nuclear waste, to stop the destruction of the ozone layer, to save the rain forests and wetlands, or to halt the totally unbalanced over-consumption by the few. Elizabeth Johnson writes: "Every year, the 20% of Earth's people in the rich nations use 75% of the world's resources and produce 80% of the world's waste."[7]

There is also a spiritual component today to the struggle of saving the earth. Time is running out and experts say that there are only 25 or 30 years left to turn the destructive spiral around. The problems are overwhelming and the laborers are few. We can organize and we can work, but the odds are against us. At such times we need to turn to the Lord for divine help. Specifically the challenge is to pray contemplatively, to face the societal "impasse," which Constance Fitzgerald in a famous article several years ago connected with the dark night of St. John of the Cross.[8] The dark night in all sectors of the person's life, whether prayer, human relationships, or working for societal renewal is characterized by impasse.

Here is an appropriate intention and motivation for the practice of Christian Meditation. This prayer cultivates one proper response to problems beyond human control. The prayer itself is trusting acceptance, silence before God, loving surrender that brings wisdom and strength. In contemplative prayer we take all our insoluble problems to God. We wait with faith and trust, hoping for the courage to change what we can and to accept what we cannot change and the discernment to know the difference. Contemplative prayer is an admission that in the end we are in the hands of God.

Some years ago the Leadership Conference of Women Religious (LCWR) promoted a year of prayer and fasting among religious and laity alike "for the healing of broken relationships wherever they exist within our church and society." They appealed specifically for contemplative prayer and provided the following rationale:

> *In the sacred space of contemplation we allow God's creativity to touch our hearts and our imaginations with intuitive, symbolic responses of loving action. We believe that in the contemplative silence we will be surprised and experience transformation. We believe in the power of prayer to free us to envision new ways of being and acting as church and as members of an earth community.*[9]

Christian Meditation is one of the ways to inspire new creative ways of dealing with the impasses of life. It will certainly strengthen us to continue the struggle and not lose heart. The popularity of contemplative prayer in general and Christian Meditation in particular in our time may well be connected with the magnitude of the problems of this age. Desert spirituality may be a special grace for a troubled, suffering world.

Endnotes

1 Adalbert de Vogüé, O.S.B., "From John Cassian to John Main: Reflections on Christian Meditation." This article in manuscript form is as yet unpublished.
2 *Tenth Conference on Prayer*, 10. 2; 10.9-10.
3 Donal O'Leary, "High Noon at Ghost Ranch," *The Furrow* 52 (2001) 27-35.
4 Dorothee Soelle, *Silent Cry: Mysticism and Resistance* (Minneapolis: Fortress Press, 2001) 88-93.
5 Cited from his *Désert Solitaire* by Thomas J.McCarthy, "The Ultimate Solution," *America* (9 April 2001) 6
6 Stephen Bede Sharper, "A New Heaven and a New Earth", *Christian Spirituality Bulletin 8 (*Fall-Winter, 2000) 15
7 "God's Beloved Creation", *America* (16 April 2001) 9
8 "Dark Night as Impasse," in *Living with Apocalypse,* ed. Tilden Edwards (San Francisco: Harper and Row, 1984)
9 "Open Letter to U.S.Catholics," *America* (19 November 2001) 17

Chapter Six

Christian Meditation as the Soul of the Apostolate

The "soul of the apostolate," in the classic text of Dom Chautard[1], is the interior life, cultivated by liturgy, mental prayer and custody of the heart. Chautard shows the organic connection between personal spiritual life and fruitful ministry. The present chapter proposes to nuance this teaching by narrowing the meaning of soul in the phrase and let it refer to spirit or the deepest part of the soul. It would mean the center of one's being, the seat of contemplation. The thesis of this chapter would then be saying that contemplative prayer, and specifically Christian Meditation is the soul of the soul of the apostolate.

The center of the soul is like the point of a cone, the still point around which the whole spiritual edifice of our lives is built and directed. It is God's dwelling place in the soul, from where God acts in us and touches all the levels of our lives. Our goal as Christians is to move ever more deeply into that space and eventually to dwell there in union with God. Contemplative prayer is the instrument to move us there, both by its own dynamism and by the fact that it affects and enhances all our spiritual activity. The deeper we have penetrated our interior depths, the more our lives are under the reign of God. Our apostolate thrives under this influence. Its effectiveness is measured by the depth of this influence. If we are coming from that deep place in our being, our ministry is suffused with God.

Contemplative prayer is a major means to deep interiority. We maintain that it is the soul of the apostolate. As such, it is the organizing principle of the interior life. It nourishes the divine presence within us and brings us ever closer to our center. In this way we are moved by the Spirit in all our choices and our actions are more and more divine. The name for this new state is contemplation; contemplative union with God. It is the measure of our worth in all our relationships, whether with God, people or the world. If we are close to God, if we possess God within ourselves, God will be in all these relationships. Contemplative prayer is not the only way to the center, but it is the most direct one and it affects everything else in our spiritual lives, including the sacraments or love of neighbor or ministry. Contemplation is nourished by faithful contemplative prayer and contemplation is the pearl of great price, our transformation in Christ.

In this age of information glut and hyperactivity, dominated by technology and the demon of busyness, contemplative prayer is counter-cultural. But scores of people have taken it up, perhaps as an antidote to the superficiality, mindlessness, and distractions of postmodern life. New contemplative prayer forms have sprung up to help people go directly to their center. William Johnston writes about this phenomenon:

> *... everywhere we see Christians of all ages and cultures sitting quietly in meditation. Some sit before a crucifix or an icon in pointed meditation. Others sit and breathe as they look at the tabernacle. Others practice mindfulness, awareness of God in their surroundings. Others recite a mantra to the rhythm of their breath. Others, influenced by Zen or yoga or* ***vipassana*** *open their minds and hearts to God in the universe.*[2]

These prayers nourish contact with God in direct and pure ways; and as such contribute in a radical way to ministry. They are exercises of the faith that does justice. Christian Meditation is our contemplative prayer form. It is not mystical or passive as such, but a self-chosen way of practicing deep silence before God, in quiet and loving awareness of the indwelling God, making ourselves vulnerable to God's action. One stands alone before God, waiting to be touched with the love poured forth into our hearts by the Holy Spirit who is given to us. (Rom 5:5)

The waiting is the contemplative prayer; the touch or inbreaking of God is contemplation. We have met this distinction many times already. Contemplative prayer is the means, contemplation the goal. The contemplation may be an ordinary grace of peaceful presence to God or the gift of infused contemplation. The prayer is positioning oneself to welcome the Spirit, the contemplation is the Spirit praying within.

Prayer and Action

Prayer in general and action for others are the two prongs of the Christian life. We have only two things to do in life: to pray and to do justice. We pray in order to know we are loved by God and, in response, to love God in return. We do justice to share that love in service to sisters and brothers. Justice embraces all our relationships; they are just when each subject receives its due.

Both elements are essential. We are called to be mystics and prophets. Mystics know God by way of love. Prophets speak up for God and do God's work. The Christian vocation is prayer and prophecy, contemplation and action, love of God and love of people. John Paul II expressed this double call beautifully in these words: "We need heralds of the gospel who are experts in humanity, who know the depths of the human heart, who can share the joys and the hopes, the agonies and distress of people today, but who are at the same time contemplatives in love with God."[3]

Activists who do not pray are do-gooders who do their own thing, often in self-serving ways. They pose a danger, which Thoreau recognized when he made the sage comment: "When you see someone coming toward you to do you good, run for your life." Rootedness in God avoids this pitfall; it promotes objectivity and selflessness. True love is other-centered, indeed God-centered, and prayer in some form is essential for this focus. People have to break out of their egoistic worlds. Prayer helps them do that. It puts them in touch with truths bigger than themselves, with Truth itself, and so it helps them be self-effacing, less aggressive, and more compassionate. Prayer helps them do God's thing rather than their own thing.

By the same token prayers can lock themselves into prayer and close their eyes to Lazarus at the gate. Such people practice a religion of comfort, as easement from the burdens of life. Theirs is a lopsided spirituality, one that is too self-regarding, too dreamy, too removed from human suffering. Spirituality helps one find meaning and acceptance even of suffering; in fact it embraces the inevitable pain of life. A mature spirituality may even go "looking for a fight," or at least accepting one when it is met, in the manner of the Good Samaritan, who did not cross by on the other side of the road. True Christians seek out hurting people and systemic injustice in order to be of help. The prophets in both covenants were on fire for the work of justice. This concern is at the heart of contemporary spirituality. The gospel is summed up in faith and justice; it is a call to change, not only ourselves, but the world.

We need to be activists who pray and prayers who do justice. This chapter addresses the first half of the equation. I write as a Carmelite, and Carmelite theory starts with prayer and moves to action. But while Carmel emphasizes the inner life, it is wholly committed to peace and justice. "The work of justice," the superior general of the Carmelites wrote in a recent circular letter, "must be an integral part of our preaching of the gospel and inform everything we do." Prayer and justice are a both-and dyad, never either-or.

Our basic assumption, then, is that ministry in general and social action in particular need prayer as a foundation and support. Christians who want to change the world according to the principles of the kingdom of God need to be guided by the gospel, not only in their heads, but in their hearts. Intellectual conversion is negotiated by study, but moral and religious conversion is the work of prayer. The prayer that changes hearts most profoundly is contemplative, for example, the Christian Meditation we are expounding.

Collaborators with God, ministers of Christ, promoters of the social mission of the Church must act out the mind of Christ. This means studying the gospel and praying it in *lectio divina.* To be committed and surrendered to the truth means to draw one's strength from the indwelling Holy Spirit. Contemplative prayer hones that connection with God. It is not enough for Christian ministers to have an Enlightenment mentality that appreciates social equality, freedom, and human progress as supreme goods, but without any higher reference to God. Earthly goods are values, but they need to be inserted into the broader picture of the redemption of the whole person. Otherwise the commitment to human progress becomes an idol; promoters easily become violent revolutionaries. A prayerful life is essential for gospel living and apostolic action.

Contemplative Prayer

The thesis of this chapter is not that contemplative prayer is the only prayer one should practice. That would smack of magic. Contemplative prayer is the centerpiece and companion to liturgy, devotions and discursive or imaginative meditation. Within the context of a healthy spiritual practice contemplative prayer is the catalyst that deepens all other prayer and insures authenticity. It puts the emphasis on the essential, the connection with the living God. That is why initiation into Christian Meditation usually involves a conversion to a more serious spiritual life in newcomers.

Christian Meditation is not a new fad or a flash in the pan that burns for the moment and then goes out. It is a long term challenge that demands faithfulness over time, and in this way it achieves a level of contemplation that is a gift for the whole community. At the same time it keeps the contemplative tradition of the church alive. It is new wine in new wineskins, but it represents an old way of life that has proven itself over the centuries in the cloister and is now being transferred into lay life. John Main saw his vocation as the call to bring the contemplative tradition of the church into the lives of the laity.[4] The contemplative movement in the church today is a lay movement and a very significant part of the post-Vatican II role of the laity in the church.

One reason for the popularity of Christian Meditation (and similar new prayer forms like Centering Prayer) is their practicality. They open up the possibility of a contemplative life for the average person of faith by teaching a simple method of prayer. The western contemplative tradition is a rich one in philosophical analyses, stages and passages, even ladders of perfection. But it has little instruction on how to get on the ladder. The "how-to" aspects seem to be ignored. Writers seemed to presume that a fervent Christian would grow into a contemplative prayer style. People would pray contemplatively when they were ready for it, and that meant they had exhausted the effectiveness of discursive prayer and now loved God enough not to need words or feelings any longer.

In this view relationship with God followed the patterns of any other love relationship. It would begin with many and long conversations, pass through periods of effusive sentiments and affections, and end up in a silent, person-to-person presence, like grandma and grandpa on the front porch, who sit together for long periods without saying a word. They did not need to talk. Each knew what the other was thinking. They had grown old in each other's love and company, and it was enough just to be together. Silent and solitary prayer was like that; it came naturally at the proper time.

The new contemplative prayer forms that are popular today anticipate this development. They go immediately and directly to the end- result of faithfulness in mental prayer. They move immediately into watching and waiting. Many Christian Meditators admit a long-standing hunger for a deeper prayer life; they have wanted to experience God, not just thoughts about him, to know God personally as friend and not just as an impersonal judge.

How to achieve this? How to get closer to God? Christian Meditation is the answer and it comes like a gift from heaven. People hear the attractive words of St. Teresa of Avila to her nuns: "Enter, then, enter within yourselves, my daughters; and get right away from your own trifling good works." [5] Enter there with your whole being - body, soul and spirit - and meet your God.

Christian Meditation is like the venerable "Jesus Prayer" of Orthodox Christianity. But it owes more to John Cassian than to Mount Athos or the Hesychasts. It is western, and has only an historical and external connection with the similar Hindu practice. John Main first practiced meditation with a mantra through his encounter with an Indian monk, Swami Satyananda. Satyananda encouraged the young John Main to choose a Christian mantra and adapt the practice to his Christian beliefs. At the time he was a colonial layman in the English diplomatic corps and working in Malaya. The Christian mantra served John well, and it was this experience that, many years later as a Benedictine monk, he found resonated with the teachings of John Cassian and *The Cloud of Unknowing*. This experience in Malaya already suggested the main lines of Christian Meditation that John Main was later to teach from his own tradition. The use of a mantra with a Christian interpretation however is not the only benefit the West has taken from the East. The East has taught the West a great deal about the role of the body at prayer, such as posture, breathing, and relaxation. Without any compromising of faith Christian Meditation has learned from the East and become a popular prayer that involves the wisdom of the centuries.[6]

Relationship to Ministry

Lectio divina, which is a spiritual reading and reflection on the Scriptures leading to prayer and contemplation, can be a valuable context for understanding Christian Meditation. The goal is the contemplation, so the movement is from discursive activity to silent presence. The *Lectio's* contemplative goal has been downplayed in the recent past, and the discursive part of the prayer has dominated Catholic piety since the anti-mystical prejudices of the 17th and 18th centuries. The revival of Christian Meditation reverses that trend. It starts and ends with a prayer of pure simplicity and thus puts contemplative prayer and contemplation back into the mainstream of Christian spirituality. Christian Meditation compliments *lectio divina* and, like a blood transfusion, it pumps new life into other ways of praying as well. It invigorates Christian life with the freshness of personal experience.

The method of Christian Meditation is the "introversion" of the western tradition, exemplified in Augustine and in the apophatic mystics. This way consists in entering into oneself. One moves within, beyond the superficial layers of the psyche, of ego, of thoughts and feelings about God, to the still point of the soul, the dwelling place of God. Beginners move in that direction; mystics touch the still point.

Social activists or busy ministers need not fear that this style of praying will remove them from the world and its concerns. This is not an introversion that leads to self preoccupation. Quite the contrary; the journey within is the journey into reality, the reality of the whole person, of humanity, and of the universe. The center holds everything, because it is my deepest self and the dwelling place of God. The more we are in touch with ourselves, the more we are in touch with God, with others and with the whole social fabric. This deep union makes us concerned about people, society, and the universe.

These insights help us understand why meditation is the helpmate of ministry. Each human being is called to hold the whole world in his/her hands. If I can offer a geometrical image; imagine a cone shape standing upside down. In the Christian life we are called to make the journey from the upper outside of the cone to the central point below. The point of the cone is the still point of the soul, the dwelling place of God and the place where we become most ourselves. The top half of the cone is our outer selves, the region of the sensibility, connecting us with the visible world. The bottom, narrowing half is our spiritual selves, where we are receptive of God's light and love and from which we can affect our choices in the upper level and outer world. We begin our journey to God on the upper level of the cone, circling around the circumference of ourselves and gradually spiraling downward to the center. The journey is the longest we will ever take, because it involves the transformation of our whole being in God. The point we are moving toward is the central meridian for the whole cone. The deeper we go, the more integrated we will have become because we have found our center.None of us is alone in the universe. We are many cones, and all of us are united together in the same one center, that is the Spirit of Christ that holds together and animates everything. The deeper our life - that is, the closer we are to the center - the more in touch we are with everyone and everything. In our spiral down to the center, the love of God and the love of neighbor work in consonance. They are the one same love with two expressions existing in the same degree of perfection. The more we love God, the more we love the world made in the image of God, and the more we are committed to making the world conform to that image.

How do we make the journey to the center? By letting go and letting God. On the ego level we think that we are in charge, that we control the operation. But analysis shows that the Spirit is leading us even here. Our task is conversion. The level of ego is also the level of the false self, which tends to construct reality according to its own image and to seek its own glory. This is the level of addictions and compulsions, hang-ups and attachments but also spiritual pride and perfectionism. We must let go of whatever imprisons us. This happens as we come to know the God of grace and unconditional love revealed in the gospels.

This involves a human effort, prompted by grace, and some use of our reason and rational activity. But then we have to shift gears and enter the region of the spirit. We have to let go into God. This is the real conversion; not our love for God but our openness to God's transforming love for us. On the spirit level God intervenes more directly and we simply receive knowledge and love. We enter this realm of freedom by the work of attention; coming to know and own the truth about ourselves and life and God. This attention to truth helps us to wake up and break the chains or the threads that hold us down and imprison us in our own brands of illusion. This is the work of purification in which God takes a direct hand by ordinary graces that we put to good usage and by mystical graces that tell us to let go and let God take over.

Full freedom will happen only when we live out of the spirit level through the gifts of the Holy Spirit. Full freedom, which is perfect poverty of spirit, is the fruit of contemplation, the work of the Holy Spirit within us. In its full realization it is a gift unearned, unmerited and joyfully received.

In active prayer we cooperate with the Spirit, using our graced human potential to grow in knowledge and love of God and to open to conversion. In Christian Meditation we are engaged in simplified active prayer, moving toward the region of the spirit, where God is the agent and we are receivers. The saying of the mantra is a work but it is a self-transcending work, not one in which we are trying to *achieve* something. It is primarily a work of attention; attention to, and celebration of, the *given-ness* of life at all levels; material, relational and mystical. The saying of the mantra begins before contemplation is 'infused' but in time it takes us beyond the self-conscious ego to a place of silence where, as John of the Cross would say, we are absorbed in God.

Christian Meditation is at home with infused contemplation, but it does not depend on it, nor does it look for it. Meditators are not likely to be concerned about naming their experience. They are busy meditating and they simply want to be lost in God. They knock at the door of the spirit level quietly, receptively, reversing the ordinary way of pursuing a goal, which is to take charge and control the outcome. Instead they reject busyness, chatter, even personal desires and feelings; their goal is relaxation before the Lord in silence, though with gentle concentration and attention, waiting on the Lord. The active-contemplative prayer leads them to the threshold of the divine presence, where hopefully they will be invited within, if not now, then when they are disposed for the gift God wishes to offer.

The experience of God has many levels and it is always by invitation only. Over time and hopefully very soon one will be invited into the mystical dwelling places of Teresa of Avila's "interior castle." But the immediate invitation is to love, not to some particular experience or even insight, according to the dictum of Teresa, that "the important thing in prayer is, not to think much, but to love much."[7] This loving is the response to being loved by God, because "the love of God consists in this, not that we have loved God, but that God has loved us." (1 John 4.10) These new contemplative prayer forms offer us the 'work' whereby, in our humanity, we can tune in directly to being the beloved children of God.

How can we nervous, distracted, anxious people silence the "chattering monkeys" of our minds and simply BE with our God? We need some method or discipline that would quiet our minds so they can dwell peacefully with the God who is present to us. This is where the mantra comes in. We also look to the East for help. We find there the wisdom of the body. In meditation we have to learn to sit still and upright, relaxed but alert. Some people find some basic stretching exercises or yoga helpful in this.

The West has tended to treat the body as the enemy; at best it paid little attention to Brother Ass. The East says the body is our friend at prayer. The body is the royal road to the spirit. Sitting upright with straight spine, breathing deeply and rhythmically, and a calmness begins to envelop your being. As Zen reminds us correct posture in Zazen is practically a guarantee of real meditation; according to these Buddhists it is enlightenment itself. In this relaxed and alert position we take up the mantra, a practice that has long been associated with the East. The mantra helps us focus and attend to the God within. We let go of all other thoughts and feelings, just noting them and letting them go. Christian Meditation repeats the mantra from beginning to end, because the mantra *is* the prayer of "selfless attention" that empties the mind in order to welcome the fullness of the divine Presence.

Why Contemplative Prayer is the Soul of the Apostolate

Christian Meditation can be a cornerstone of the spirituality of any demanding ministry, especially social action. The reasons for this position have been suggested throughout this discussion, and now we will sum up the argument in three considerations.

The first is that contemplative prayer is the very heart and soul of all prayer. C.S. Lewis says that prayer is either contact with God or sheer illusion. Prayer is dialogue, conversation, encounter, all qualities of any personal prayer. The ultimate fruit of *lectio divina,* for example, is the fourth act, which is contemplation, and the melody of that swan-song underlies the earlier discursive acts as well. Christian Meditation sets its sights immediately and directly on contemplative presence as the goal. It quiets the mind and waits in simplicity for the God who will surely come. The habit of the contact remains after the exercise and underlies our liturgical and vocal prayer and our loving response to our neighbor in need.

A story appeared in the London *Tablet* some years ago helps locate the essence of prayer. The Archbishop of Canterbury was being interviewed on television and he was asked about his prayer. "Do you pray?" was the question. "Yes," he answered, "I pray each day." "And how much do you pray?" He answered: "About a minute." There was surprise on the interviewer's face, so the archbishop added: "Of course, it takes me about 29 minutes to get to that one minute." Formal meditation periods in the classic writers on the subject since the 16th century were always set at an hour or at least a half-hour's length, because that amount of time was thought to be normal for entering deeply into one's self. Christian Meditation follows this rule, though it is a little more optimistic about the time needed.

This contemplative experience is difficult to describe. It is no one particular experience, because it is a matter of being more than intentional activity. Sometimes the resonances are consoling, warm, euphoric; more often they are matter of fact, even a "nothing experience," dry and empty. The essential is none of these feelings, but loving faith, open and receptive to God's love. There is usually no perceptible awareness of the action of the Spirit.

Therese of Lisieux may help us here. The contemplative prayer of her years in the convent was seldom self-validating. It was presence to Jesus in pure faith without any sensible overflow of consolation. Whatever delight there was in the prayer was spiritual and based on the faith conviction that she was pleasing God and wanted to be raised up in love for God. The prayer itself was dry and empty, but she knew she was loving the Beloved and drawing strength from the encounter. It was a discipline and love offering.

Most of that time she sensed that God was hidden behind a cloud or asleep in the boat with his disciples. (Luke 8:22-25) This was a presence in absence, which is the typical experience of the "dark night" in St. John of the Cross. But even this silent presence disappeared in the last year and a half of her life, when Therese had no sense whatever of a world beyond the senses. The pious thoughts of the past now seemed like illusions. She experienced total absence of God without alloy. There was no sense of God, no feeling for heaven or the once familiar world of grace. Therese offered her own explanation of this horrible suffering:

> *[Your child] is resigned to eat the bread of sorrow as long as You desire it; she does not wish to rise up from the table filled with bitterness at which poor sinners are eating until the day set by You. Can she not say in her name and in the name of her brothers, 'Have pity*

on us, O Lord, for we are poor sinners!' [Luke 18.13] Oh! Lord, send us away justified. May all those who were not enlightened by the bright flame of faith one day see it shine.[8]

She experienced the plight of sinners and atheists, their "night of nothingness," which is the reality of their condition.[9] They do not feel the pain; they live in denial and avoidance through medicating themselves with distractions or drugs and substituting ersatz gods. But Therese experienced the full force of their nihilistic state; she took on their pain in redemptive suffering. Here as in all her prayer life Therese understood the value of poverty of spirit. She wrote the following words to her sister Marie: "Let us love our littleness, let us love to feel nothing; then we shall be poor in spirit, then Jesus shall come to look for us and transform us into flames of love." [10]

Poverty of spirit is the measuring stick of the contemplation. God comes to the poor, the *anawim* of God like Mary in the *Magnificat.* (Luke 1:46-55) He touches them from his dwelling place in the depths of their souls. God is always there in the center; God is present to us, but we are not present to God. We must journey inward, passing through layers of obstruction and letting go of hang-ups and attachments, pride and perfectionism. The Spirit leads in this journey. The end is full presence in the still point, the goal which is intimacy, identification and transforming union with God. There finally is total and continuous presence with the Lord.

A brief glance at the seven mansions of St Teresa might be helpful: The earlier dwelling places, one to three, do not have a direct and immediate touching of God. The experience in the early mansions is something less and represents a peaceful resting in God from a distance, with a presence to God rather than in God. These experiences are the expectations of beginners in the practice of Christian Meditation. With growth they will be exchanged for intermittent but real encounters with the still point along the way. These are described by St Teresa in the fourth to sixth dwelling places of the *Interior Castle.*

The seventh and last mansion is the transforming union. Only at the end of the journey is there full possession of God in the still point. Then the "spark," as the still point is also called, will burst into the living flame of love.

Contemplative prayer is the pursuit of the Beloved. Its strategy is to make oneself vulnerable as possible to the divine inbreaking. Contemplative prayer lives in the hope that God will come, indeed is coming, whatever the emotional overtones of the time at prayer. Those who practice this prayer are convinced that there are breakthroughs all along the way. They know that God is always ready to give himself to those disposed.

Discernment

A second reason for promoting contemplative prayer in ministry is discernment. This prayer is a direct way to the truth of things. In this prayer one is reduced to silence, beyond our self-serving thoughts and feelings. Silence is the way to truthfulness. Our true self comes to life. This is the self that is rooted in God; it comes from God and leads back to God. It is our real self, not the one we have fashioned according to our own image and likeness. Whatever the level of the contemplation enjoyed in the practice of the contemplative prayer, it will be an experience in some fashion of this true self.

Christian Meditation contributes to the growth of the true self in multiple ways. The false self is sidelined; it withers from being neglected and overshadowed. But it is also laid bare and revealed as the enemy of one's deeper truth. We are easily victimized by the sin in our lives and in the world. The capital sins, for example, spawn desires of pride, lust, avarice and the rest. Our own efforts to deal with these things are only partially successful, according to St John of the Cross,[11] because the capital sins continue their disruptive action from the underground of the unconscious; they are part of the person's shadow. They come out in disguised forms such as spiritual pride or gluttony. Contemplation uncovers this pathology and challenges the persons to own their sins and to deal with them, by facing and accepting them in times of formal prayer and by actively dealing with them in a proper forum after prayer in a program like the 12 Steps. This healing process is the purification described by John of the Cross as the dark night of the senses. Only contemplation can heal the roots of sin. It does this by revealing faults in their true colors and by mustering the strength to deal with them effectively. This process of purification is happening often without awareness in practitioners of contemplative prayer.

As purification takes place, a new consciousness emerges, which Meister Eckhart calls *Gelassenheit*. This term means "letting things be," seeing things as they are, reading the situation accurately without projection. *Gelassenheit* happens when the person is connected with the living God and lets other gods die. It is the outcome of detachment; it is the reward of seeing the world with the eyes of faith. This frame of mind helps one choose the right course of action. Social analysis and inquiry into each situation are still necessary, but *Gelassenheit* assures greater objectivity and truth.

Contemplative prayer is also the handmaid of spiritual discernment in another way. Spiritual discernment proceeds less by way of rational analysis than by connaturality, that is, by affective consonance or dissonance with a given experience. One interprets the affective resonances of the experience. The discerner "senses" what is in accord with or in opposition to God's will. The judgment is by a "feel" for the truth. There is affinity for the good in the way a chaste person knows intuitively what is or is not the chaste thing. Spiritual discernment of this type is possible only for a spiritual person, one who cultivates a deep and faithful prayer life, is close to God, and has grown to think and judge like God. Christian Meditation fosters that kind of likeness.

It puts one in contact with the Spirit and brings forth the harvest of virtuous attitudes described by St. Paul as fruits of the Spirit: "love, peace, patient endurance, kindness, generosity, faith." (Gal 5.22) These are qualities of true Christian ministers who are motivated not by ideology, but by the Spirit of God, who is working in them for the building up of the kingdom of God.

Personal Relationship

The third and final reason for recommending this prayer as the keystone of one's prayer life and the ideal preparation for ministry is its personal quality. Christian Meditation brings about a truly personal relationship with Jesus Christ. Jesus walks at one's side as friend and support, reminding us that he is in charge, that it is his church, and that we are not the ones finally responsible. The mantra becomes like a friend or loved ones name that comes to mind in moments of quiet or crisis and calls up the Lord's presence. There is a sense of intimacy between God and the person.

With contemplative prayer as a regular practice there is less danger that the "first and greatest" commandment will be ignored. Today the very possibility of a personal relationship with God is often cast into doubt. Love for God is flattened out into horizontal expressions among people, the love of God is a phrase that really means loving people.[12] To love another person is indeed to love God himself, but this is the secondary expression of the love of God; the first way is to love God in God's very self. Loving God himself, who is Abba, our mother and father, or Jesus, the Word Incarnate, or Holy Spirit, the God in us are our birthright as Christians. We are called to a Person-to-person relationship with each member of the Trinity: this is the ultimate purpose of life and the measure of its fulfillment. We are called to be friends, not mere servants (John 15:15), to dwell like branches on the vine who is Jesus. Jesus says: "I pray that all may be one as you, Father, are in me, and I in you, I pray that they may be one in us." (John 17:21) Christian Meditation cultivates this personal relationship that mystics have called 'indwelling'.

One especially important role for this personal friendship with Christ is in the area of suffering. Jesus is no stranger to suffering. In his earthly life he sought out and befriended the downtrodden and the hurting. Their needs are still his preferential option. We should not be surprised to find suffering in our ministry, since we act in imitation of him. The Cross is the validation of all Christian life and ministry. It is part of the human condition and the paschal mystery of dying and rising with Christ. So there will be the Cross in ministerial life, suffered in failures and opposition, in boredom and discouragement, in sheer weariness and disappointment, in persecution and even martyrdom. How shall ministers manage this fearsome challenge? With Paul we ask: "Who can rescue me from this body of death?" The answer too is Paul's: "Thanks be to God through Jesus Christ." (Rom 7:24-25 NRSV)

One especially efficacious form of the grace of Christ in ministry is the experience of his personal presence in our lives. The faithful practice of Christian Meditation builds that sense of abiding presence, that knowing Christ by name, that intimacy of walking with him. There are no doubt other ways of growing in the knowledge and love of the Lord, but the way of contemplative prayer goes to the heart of the matter. It is a special gift for our time and the guarantee of a solid spiritual foundation for ministry. For those who take up its practice it will be the soul of their apostolate.

Endnotes

1 Dom Jean-Baptiste Chautard, O.C.S.O., *The Soul of the Apostolate* (translated with introduction by Thomas Merton: Image paperback, l961)
2 *Mystical Theology* (London: Harper-Collins, 1995) 134.
3 Address to Sixth Symposium of European Bishops, 1985
4 The genesis and development of John Main's vocation to renew the contemplative mission of the Church is described by L. Freeman in his introduction to *John Main, Essential Writings* (Maryknoll:Orbis, 2002), especially 28-40.
5 *Interior Castle, Third Dwelling Places* 1.4 (E. Allison Peers translation).
6 William Johnston, S.J., *op.cit.,* 134 calls the contemporary contemplative prayer neither western or eastern, but "a third way, a *tertium quid.* It is the Gospel of Jesus Christ in a new world."
7 *Interior Castle, IV Dwelling Places,* 1.7 in Kieran Kavanaugh/Otilio Rodrigez translation, (Washington: Institute of Carmelite Studies, 1980) 319.
8 *Story of a Soul* (tr. John Clarke, O.C.D.: Washington: Institute of Carmelite Studies, 1975) 212.
9 *Ibid*, 213.
10 *Letters of St. Therese of Lisieux*, II, LT l97 , September 17, 1896, (tr. John Clarke, O.C.D.: Washington: Institute of Carmelite Studies, l988) 999.
11 *Dark Night*, I, 2-8.
12 Edward Vacek, S.J., "Religious Life and the Eclipse of Love" for *Review for Religious* 57 (March-April, 1998) 118-137; also "The Eclipse of Love of God," *America* 174 (1996) 15-16.

Chapter Seven

Aspiratory Prayer, A Complement to Christian Meditation

John Main's rediscovery of meditation with a mantra in the Christian tradition began in the early 1970s. As a Benedictine monk he was, for a while, headmaster of the school at St. Anselm's Abbey in Washington DC. A student who had been traveling in India and staying in ashrams learning meditation and yoga came to St. Anselm's to enquire about Christian mysticism. As is usual in monasteries the busiest person gets given new tasks and John Main was given the task of answering this boy's enquiries. He gave the boy a book that is a classic of the English Benedictine tradition, though seldom read even in monasteries: Dom Augustine Baker's *Holy Wisdom*. Written at the end of the sixteenth century, it was a call to contemplative renewal within the monasteries. The ancient tradition of monastic prayer had all but disappeared at that time.

Baker's book is not an easy read and John Main had hoped this would keep the student busy for some time and may put him off from coming back at all. To John Main's surprise few days later the student returned enthused by what he had read, saying it was the same as what he had learned about meditation at the ashrams. John Main was reminded of his own experience in Malaya where he had learned to meditate using a Christian mantra. When he had joined the monastery he was told to give up this practice as 'not-Christian'. Could it be that here in Baker there were signs of a long neglected Christian tradition of meditation? John Main began to read the text along with his student companion and there he discovered Baker's teaching on 'aspirative prayer' or 'aspirations'. He also discovered Baker's references to an even older tradition of monologistic prayer from the Desert Fathers. John Main felt he had come home to the mantra at the very heart of monastic identity.

Aspirative prayer or aspirations, for Augustine Baker, are fervent desires of the heart expressing love of God and desire for his love. "My God, I love you" is an aspiration or the single phrase "My God and my all" that St. Francis of Assisi was noted to pray all through the night. They are expressed in words, or sighs, or silence. To aspire means to breathe, with the connotation of breathing hard for something. In aspiratory prayer one breathes out heartfelt desires for God. One yearns for God and reaches out to him. Baker links this to the earlier monastic teaching of John Cassian. In Cassian the emphasis is on poverty of spirit, the prayer phrase was repeated so that, "after saying it over and over again, after meditating upon it without pause, it has the strength to reject and refuse all the abundant riches of thought". Grasping the poverty of this little verse it will come all the more easily to that first of the Beatitudes: "Blessed are the poor in spirit for theirs is the kingdom of God."[1]

In terms of John Main's own re-discovery of the mantra, the teaching on aspirative prayer may have a close affinity with Christian Meditation. Baker's particular approach to aspirative prayer is apophatic. He writes that: "There remains in the soul and mind a nothing and a mere emptiness. This nothing is the rich inheritance of perfect souls."

Baker goes on to describe how the aspiration deepens and becomes more rooted, more subtle and pure. He says that there is an infinite progress of purity and subtlety in this state. This is the highest state – beyond this there is no spirituality but there is an infinite scope for deepening and perfecting.[2]

There is another stream of contemplation flowing from the desert where aspirative prayer is more 'affective' in its intent. For John Main, Baker and *The Cloud* author, the emotive quality of the phrase was a stepping-stone to the 'pure prayer' of the early monks, the prayer of simple regard or 'attention'. However in the Carmelite tradition aspirative prayer has a long pedigree also and is more an expression of longing, of passionate desire and of active 'intention'. The question is, can these disciplines of prayer be mutually enhancing? Are they complementary? Or is it better to respect differences of tradition and temperament, follow one's chosen path and not muddy the waters with comparison?

However, some things can be said. Firstly historically both prayers have the same roots in the western mystical tradition. Carmelite authorities like Henry Herp (d1477) and John of St. Samson (d.1636) cite the same sources of the Desert Fathers to establish the lineage of Aspirations as Baker and John Main do for the ancestry of Christian Meditation. The architects of both traditions considered monologistic prayer as a short cut, a direct route, to intimacy and oneness with God. Both stress frequent repetition of a simple phrase. In Aspirative prayer the phrase is seen as expressive of an intense desire; in the monastic tradition it is more a way of mindfulness, an object of focus and a practice of the presence of God.

In terms of practice they could be complementary: Aspirative prayer would add a strong affective component to Christian Meditation. It cultivates a warm, human approach to God, emphasizing the role of the heart in interior prayer. But then so does Christian Meditation. There is a slight difference of emphasis though: In the monastic tradition the heart is considered the center of the human person. If purified of images, the heart is the place where we 'see' God. For the Carmelite tradition, the heart is above all the place of love, the place of 'relationship' with God. Aspirations tend therefore to have an emotive quality. The older monastic tradition stresses rather a depth of awareness, often called 'dispassion'. Christian Meditation would therefore remind us not to be dependant on our 'feelings' in prayer; prayer goes on, and is often at its purest, when one feels nothing.

This reminds one that there are differences of interpretation even within the Carmelite teaching on Aspirative prayer. One group of proponents follow Henry Herp in holding that it belongs only in the journey to divine union and cedes its place when unitive love is achieved, when the goal of union with God is reached. In this case it belongs to the way and not to the term. On the other hand, one of its foremost teachers, the Venerable John of St. Samson, a Carmelite of the Ancient Observance and leader in the Reform of Touraine in 17th century France, believes that aspiratory prayer continues into the mystical state and takes on a mystical form. Always and everywhere however Aspirative prayer is associated with a passionate love of God, one that is possible only to humans and not to angels, because it includes the emotional and sensible factor.

Aspirations or aspiratory prayer was a treasure in European Christianity in the late Middle Ages and one of the great legacies of the Touraine Reform. This reform took place in "les Grandes Carmes," the popular name in France for the Carmelites of the Ancient Observance (O.Carm.). The doctrine of Aspiratory prayer has been relegated to history for many Christians today, and they neither know about it nor practice it. This is a loss for Christian spirituality.

The present chapter hopes to take one step toward correcting this oversight. The thesis of the chapter is that Aspiratory prayer can be a helpful introduction to Christian Meditation and offer the element of fire and passion to the spiritual lives of those who practice contemplative prayer.

The chapter gives an overview of what the prayer is. Then it highlights three of its outstanding proponents, the Carthusian, Hugh of Balma (13th C), the Franciscan, Henry Herp (d.1477), and the Carmelite John of St. Samson (d.1636). Finally it makes some practical suggestions on reviving the practice and connecting it with Christian Meditation.

What Is Aspiratory Prayer?

Aspiratory prayer is focused on love as desire, though in the beginning it may cover a wide sweep of emotions and feelings. Practice simplifies and unifies the faculties into the single outreaching of love, the central act of the Christian life and the form of all the virtues. Aspirations are like Christian Meditation's prayer of simplicity; both consolidate the multiple affections of affective prayer into a single attitude that has only one goal, divine union. Both prayer forms emphasize love. The teaching of Christian Meditation draws on the 14th century English treatise *The Cloud of Unknowing* which says that "God cannot be known by thought but only by love". Both reach out to God beyond the discursive intellect. Though God is unknown, aspirations are based on the infinite attractiveness of God. He draws our love. This is similar to what John Main said about meditation that it is "as natural to the spirit as breathing is to the body".

Catholic teachers in the past were sticklers in assessing the degrees of prayer and assigning them to their proper stage of growth. The prayer of beginners was discursive meditation, which emphasized reason and reflection. The second stage was the heart's domain, and therefore affective prayer or the pouring out of many affections. The third stage was contemplative prayer. This was one, long act of love, like looking lovingly at the tabernacle. The peasant in the story associated with the Cure d'Ars' prayed this way and described his prayer in the well-known words: "I look at Him and He looks at me."

In practice however these are not linear and many people come to Christian Meditation without prior preparation in discursive or affective prayer. Aspirative prayer is however dependant on some prior engagement of the affections with God. Christian Meditation (along with similar methods) has democratized contemplative prayer today and encouraged its practice in a wide selection of people. For the practice of contemplative prayer, some knowledge and love of the Lord is necessary, but less knowledge and love than was thought necessary in the past. Just as there has been a tendency in Christianity to reserve mystical prayer for an elite so also there has been a tendency to identify the spiritual with immaterial and corresponding denigration of the bodily.[3] The World Community of Christian Meditation reminds us that the depth of contemplative prayer is open to people of all walks of live, married or single, in monasteries or running businesses.

Aspirative prayer similarly is an antidote and corrective against exaggerated spiritualism and minimizing the bodily. It is patently passionate and embraces the emotional and the sensible order. It is intensely human and welcomes expressions of love that include the sensual element of passion, so much so that some of its teachers taught that aspirations are always sensible-spiritual love and never purely spiritual love. Aspirations belong to the body-soul composite and are not at home with angelic loves. They put a human stamp, not only on the love of God, but on contemplation itself, emphasizing love over knowledge, the heart over the head.[4]

Aspiratory prayer comes out of the same milieu as Christian Meditation. Christian Meditation is a well-defined discipline of prayer, a contemporary re-presentation from the western contemplative tradition. No such development has taken place for aspiratory prayer. It is a free-floating way of relating to God that is adaptable alongside other prayer forms and, I feel, compatible with Christian meditation. It could even serve to enrich the teaching of John Main by linking it up with another ancient tradition of monologistic prayer. Seeing the mantra as a prayer of praise could also enhance John Main's teaching on 'the practice of the presence of God'. 'Maranatha' is both an invocation, "Come, Lord", and a celebration, "the Lord comes!" Authors seeking to authenticate either of these two systems of prayer appeal to the same sources, even the same texts in tradition.

Christian Meditation seeks silent presence and quiet resting in God. At the same time it is active prayer, rightly called meditation, but in a non-discursive or contemplative mode. It is not classical contemplation in the sense of infused prayer received passively, but the work of human effort combined with grace. Aspiratory prayer is obviously active in the same sense. It uses the language of intense, passionate love and expresses yearning of the heart and delight in resting in the Lord. Aspiratory prayer is more than loving conversation with God. It expresses an outreach of love and desire for God. So it is more than a tête-à-tête, even in the loving language of affective colloquy. The difference is intensity. General affective prayer (such as devotions, meditations on the passion or emotive passages from scripture) engages the feelings but in varied and diffuse ways, whereas urgent longings for intimacy dominate aspiratory prayer.

Aspirations fit nicely into the perspectives and practice of "love mysticism," which is a form of relating to God in spousal love. The language of spousal love is very human, amorous, and erotic. Its biblical source is *The Song of Songs* or *Hosea* as well as John's gospel and some of Paul's letters, and it flourished in medieval women like Mechthild of Magdeburg and Hadewijch of Brabant as well as in men like St. Bernard and St. John of the Cross. Janet K. Ruffing has written a guide for the spiritual direction of those called this way and cites examples from history and her own case studies of its passionate experience and language.[5] Elizabeth Dreyer has written a well-researched study of the topic, called *Passionate Spirituality.*[6] Pope Benedict XVI has written sensitively about the role of eros in the formation of the love of God in his first encyclical, *Deus Caritas Est.*

The practice of aspirative prayer is not limited to spousal love. It is at home with a more practical charity that is described as filios or friendship in the teaching of Thomas Aquinas. Still the normal form of Aspiratory prayer is sensible-spiritual love, and for Henry Herp this is its only legitimate expression. Aspirative prayer in Herp's view is emotional and passionate by definition. A purely spiritual form is recognized by John of St. Samson, but Herp prefers to call this follow-up form unitive love. For John of St. Samson, pure spiritual love is a mystical form of aspiration, and it leads one into the furnace of God's love and continues in transforming union. For both authors the will is the driving force in all fervent expression of love of God; the will is not surrendered but is actively engaged in seeking the one it loves.

A parallel and contrast can be seen here with the teaching of *The Cloud of Unknowing* that has been so formative in the understanding of Christian Meditation. *The Cloud* author was writing a century before Henry Herp and is a classic of English spirituality. He was writing at a time when sensible-spiritual experience of God had become all the vogue through the influence of Richard Rolle. The mysticism of *The Cloud of Unknowing* features a whole-hearted love but less obvious passionate. The author is concerned that God is loved purely, for what and who God is, and not for any 'experience' we might have of God's love. He was worried about the dangers of seeking any sensible-spiritual experience through the body or even the emotions. Following a strict apophatic path *The Cloud* teaches that both thought and feeling are limited to what God reveals of God's self. Revelation and devotion are not something we can think or feel by our own effort of intellect and will, they are gifts. Furthermore *The Cloud* encourages the true contemplative to be 'stripped bare' of thought and feeling so as to love the giver and not only the gift. The will has to be purified in its intent.

The teaching on Aspirative prayer does recognize this. The expression of loving desires for God continues in down days and dryness as much as in times of sweetness and sensible consolation. It does not presuppose a spiritual high. However the feeling element is still there; it is genuine and authentic, not faked or pretended or forced. Therese of Lisieux is a perfect example of the expression of passionate desires of love for God in the darkest moments of life.[7] There are degrees in the practice that correspond to the person's habitual love of God but in the end the Carmelite tradition recognizes that it is not we who pray. The aspiration ceases to be an act of the will and, as John of St. Samson writes beautifully, it becomes rather a mystical expression in which the Holy Spirit breathes out enflamed desires for God.

History and Theology of Aspiratory Prayer

Aspiratory prayer flourished in the late Middle Ages in northern Europe, especially in the Rhineland and France from the 13th to the 17th century. At the time of the Touraine Reform the practice was common in popular religious culture. Aspirative prayer appealed to the architects of Touraine, because they saw the practice as dovetailing with their view of the goal of the Carmelite Order, which was to live continuously in the loving presence of God. Intimations of aspiratory prayer are found in the New Testament, the contemporaries, St. Augustine and John Cassian, St. Benedict, and Guigo II, and others. The first to give aspirative prayer a central place in the spiritual life was Hugh of Balma, whose Theologia Mystica exerted wide influence, partly because it was thought to be the work of St. Bonaventure. Hugh of Balma taught the way of the heart, and aspiratory prayer was its chief expression. First one must know one's weak self and the goodness of God, since anyone filled with self is unable to yearn for God. This knowledge prepares one to rise up to God in "anagogic contemplation".

Anagogic contemplation means moving from creature to Creator, for example, from the text of Scripture to the living God, and in Hugh of Balma with a heart inflamed with desire and love. Such is his concept of aspiratory prayer. In Hugh the love is either natural-spiritual, which is the equivalent of sensible-spiritual love, or purely spiritual where God is the direct object like in *The Cloud*. The love increases with the simplification and unification of the faculties until ultimately there is mystical union with the Trinity in the high point of the soul called the "*apex mentis*." Henry Herp and John of St. Samson will pick up on these views and expand them by putting them in the framework of Jan van Ruusbroec's theology (d.1381).

Hugh had many imitators, especially among the Carthusians, who promoted and developed this teaching so effectively, that it became "the Carthusian method of prayer" and moved Mercurian, an early general of the

Jesuits, to warn the Society that it was a competitor that could marginalize Ignatian prayer in Spain.[8] *The Cloud of Unknowing,* is likely a Carthusian document[9] and can easily be read as a treatise on aspiratory prayer, even though the name is not used.

Henry Herp, O.F.M. (d.1447)

Henry Herp has written the first synthesis of the whole spiritual journey around the topic of Aspirative prayer. His map is the structure of the soul as delineated by the great Flemish mystical writer Jan van Ruusbroec. The soul is three concentric circles, each of them representing a different level of human activity. Herp offers a detailed plan for moving through the outer two levels and arriving at the inner circle of highest union with the Holy Trinity. He lays down instructions for each of the phases of the journey, but his chief contribution is to show how aspirative prayer moves one through the middle circle. Ruusbroec calls the three circles "spheres" or "unities," whereas Herp names them mansions or dwelling places like Teresa of Avila. The first is the region of the senses, the second that of the spirit and the third the "fond" or ground, the dwelling place of the Holy Trinity.

One must traverse each level to get to the center and the way is introversion, being restored to oneself, a concept that goes back to St. Augustine. Herp also calls it "ascension". Persons "ascend" in that they are carried beyond themselves toward the center of all things. The self, as St. Augustine says, becomes a stepping stone whereby we are able to raise ourselves towards God. The searcher leaves behind the lesser level or a part of it in favor of the higher one. For Herp it is the process of introversion that makes the powers on each level converge toward the center and draws them into the next step. In this imagery the outer circle of exterior behavior is drawn inwards into the middle circle, and in the middle the lower interior faculties of the irascible and concupiscible appetites, the reason and free will are introverted into the spiritual faculties of intellect, memory and will. These latter will finish the task of journeying into God and will in turn be drawn into mystical union in the center. At each stage Herp points out that the imagery of ascension could also be used, the soul being concentrated in itself and thus 'raised' toward God.

The introversion or ascension starts with the outer or exterior circle, which represents the active life. The means set down by Herp for this first introversion are "truth and compassion." Truth means understanding the goodness of God and the bankruptcy of the human, and compassion is appreciating God's love and attractiveness. It is interesting to see how positive is the understanding of Herp on beginnings. The middle level is the field for aspiratory prayer and unitive love. Aspirations come from the "interior inferior powers," especially the concupiscible appetite, which in Herp's view has a spiritual quality about it. Unitive love is exercised by the spiritual faculties.

Understanding guides the process, hence the value of regular reflection as well as the repetition of a prayer phrase that recalls the supreme attraction of God and draws the soul in love. The awakened will moves the sensory faculties to yearn for God, progressively spiritualizing the person for the work of unitive love. Unitive love for Herp takes over from the lower interior faculties and replaces aspirations. The acts of pure, unitive love finish the task of the introversion/ascension of the spirit level and lead into the center, where the love is fruitive. The middle, aspirative way is left behind and the soul now lives the "super-essential life" of oneness with the Trinity (a union that for most Christian mystics is psychological not ontological).

Herp offers some good pastoral advice. Aspiratory prayer often begins with rote expressions of love and fervor, at times a simple repetition of intent. According to Herp these outreachings will in time lead to a genuine feeling of love. This, he says, has its own danger of entrapping the person in delightful, sensible sweetness so the love is gradually purified and becomes the unitive love that will lead the soul into the center. Unitive love too undergoes its own purifications, which may entail experiences as dark and dry as the initial entry was exalted. The challenge at this point, as at every point in the spiritual life, is putting the self in its place, that is, letting go of everything that is not God. The holy soul practicing spiritual love will continue to work at the total gift of self to God, and its tasks are listed by Herp as self-offering, searching for God's will, letting God's love destroy all defects, and being united with God.

John of St. Samson (d.1636)

John of St. Samson is an immensely important figure in the Carmel of the Ancient Observance. He was a mystic of profound experience and in spite of the blindness that afflicted him from the age of three he was well educated and well read, keeping in touch with currents of spirituality in the very rich 17th century. He has been called the French John of the Cross and is highly esteemed by religious historians like Henri Bremond and Louis Cognet.

John of St. Samson lived a century and a half after Herp, but Herp's work was well-known to him in the numerous Latin and French translations and in the plethora of spiritual writings that popularized aspiratory prayer. John of St. Samson became expert in the teaching of this way, building on Herp but adding his own points of view. There had been a lot of writing, but little development since Herp. After a careful comparison of the two authors the Carmelite scholar Cornelius Janssen concludes John's doctrine is Herp in new packaging. "Certain things have been left out," he writes, "others developed; in short the whole has acquired a new face." [10]

John belongs to the same Dutch school of mysticism as Herp; both of them appropriating the theology of Ruusbroec. We come from God as created images in the Uncreated Word, and our life goal is to return to our place in the Word in full consciousness of our unity in God. The goal is put rather abstractly as "the state of consummation of the subject in the Object" in a "union without difference or distinction". Such is the transforming union, in which the soul is caught up in the fire of the divine life. The way to the goal is introversion/ascension according to the same divisions as those of Henry Herp, but with adaptations in nomenclature.

John is particularly eloquent is explaining how spiritual love guides the whole process of introversion/ascension once aspirations become the way. Spiritual love is at the heart of sensible-spiritual aspirations and it constitutes the spiritual aspirations themselves that lead one into the center. Aspirations have the genius of putting our full humanity to work by engaging our feelings and emotions as well as our spirit. Sensible love is the starter and it houses the spiritual love in the first expressions, which are sensible-spiritual aspirations. When the aspirations become "more vigorous, more on fire, and more detached from sense," they are pure spiritual love. This spiritual love, with or without a sensible component, is the engine that drives the introversion/ascension process into the furnace that is God. Aspirations thus have a mystical quality in John as is clear from the following quotation:

> *Aspiration is not only an affectionate colloquy... It is a loving and inflamed transport of the whole heart and the spirit, by which the soul transcends itself and everything created and unites itself tightly with God in the liveliness of loving expression. Thus essentially expressed it goes beyond any sensible, reasonable, intellectual, or comprehensible love and through the impetuosity of the Spirit of God and one's own effort it reaches the divine union, not in limited fashion, but by a sudden transformation of the spirit in God. The spirit, I say, surpasses in itself every knowable and intelligible love in the abundant and ineffable sweetness of God himself, in whom one is lovingly embraced. Such is essential aspiration in itself, in its cause, and in its effect.* [11]

In the beginning there will be multiplicity of thoughts and feelings, but with growth this richness will give way to ever increasing simplicity and a state of pure elevation in God. Intensity is of the essence, since only strong love can break the attachments of the faculties to their natural objects. Frequency is a necessary quality, since the goal is to make aspirations come forth as from second nature; they are as natural as breathing. Humility too is the essential underpinning of all true love. But in all these efforts balance and moderation must prevent any violence or excessive force. John of St. Samson, experienced spiritual director, has good advice on how to begin and how to grow in this beautiful practice, and his reflections will help us put our topic in perspective.

When to begin? Brother John sees aspirations as a higher form of prayer, hence he is hesitant to promote the practice indiscriminately. Aware of the dangers of too much emotionality as well as its necessary pre-dispositions, he counsels against beginning the prayer prematurely. Strain and force must be resisted lest there be physical or psychological harm. It is necessary to guard against a too sanguine assessment of one's love of God. The apostle Peter felt a great love for Jesus that led to presumption and the denial of Jesus in the courtyard. John feels that candidates for this prayer should have spent "a good year" in discursive meditation and affective prayer before taking up aspirations. He warns newcomers that beginnings will be troublesome, even painful, but practice will make perfect. He was writing at a time when entrance to contemplative prayer was more guarded than it is today. However his modest assessment of the time needed for preparation shows that progression into monologistic prayer can be quite quick.

Aspiratory Prayer and Christian Meditators

It remains to suggest ways in which this body of teaching can be put into practice in people committed to the practice of Christian Meditation.

Firstly, just an awareness that, as Christian meditators, we are praying within a very broad tradition. This tradition has its varieties; John Main centered his teaching on that of John Cassian and *The Cloud of Unknowing* but there are parallels in Carmelite spirituality. Meditation and Aspirative prayer both move beyond thought and image. This may be desert spirituality but monologistic prayer is not a lone voice in the desert.

Secondly, it is not just the similarities but the differences that are important. The monastic tradition stresses more the 'purity' of prayer and helps to critique the emphasis on desire and will in Aspirative prayer, the Carmelite tradition stresses more the 'intensity' of prayer and helps to remind us that it is love that is the energy of prayer, its motivating force and its end. These are complementary as love must be pure of selfish desire as much as purity must be a state of loving self-gift.

However, that having been said, I believe the path of Christian Meditation and Aspirative prayer should not be confused so that the integral nature of the teaching that underpins them is lost. This is especially true when it comes to actual practice of a methodology of prayer. We have to be selective and not mix-and-match. Prayer is a discipline of self-transcendence and this only works if we dedicate ourselves to a path whole heartedly.

The question is: Can these ways be practiced together? My feeling is no, not at the same time, because both the logic and the method is integral to each. However I do feel they can be practiced at different times. The teaching on Christian Meditation is based on two half hours of sitting, morning and evening, where one stays with 'the grand poverty' of the mantra, as Cassian puts it. Aspirative prayer, as it is presented in the Carmelite literature, is more something that can be practiced throughout the day as a way of remembering God. This venerable Carmelite practice means to murmur aspirations frequently during the course of the day, either at set intervals like the striking of the clock or whenever one is moved to recall the presence of God, like when waiting for a bus, or involved in a task. [12] It can be the same mantra as the one used for sitting meditation or other ones, and again the flexibility of Aspirative responses may make different phrases appropriate for different circumstances, and impromptu impulses of praise, during the day.

That being said some may feel it possible to introduce Aspirative prayer into our practice of Christian Meditation. This will be adding a stronger affective dimension to the loving attention already present in the non-discursive Christian Meditation. To be faithful to the method of Christian Meditation the mantra, which is usually "maranatha", will have to carry this new affective element. The mantra will be the vehicle expressing love and desire in a more pronounced way. The mantra must remain the only articulated aspiration and its original function of cultivating poverty of spirit and selfless attention on God must not be compromised. Otherwise aspiratory prayer is replacing Christian Meditation. The aspirative intention must not disturb the repose and quiet of the contemplative prayer, but simply heighten the love that is implicit in the mantra. The aspirations in other words will not have their own independent expression; they will be silent and wordless accompaniments to the mantra and will add warmth and fervor to the prayer.

A caveat is in order. Aspirative prayer, especially in its sensible-spiritual form, is busier and engages the rational faculties more than Christian Meditation does. Introducing fervent desires and acts of love could disrupt the peaceful flow of the mantra and distract the meditator with too many thoughts and feelings. The proposed addition must reinforce and not become a parallel movement to the Christian Meditation. Otherwise the addition would be counter-productive.

A third way to practice aspiratory prayer would be to develop an extended, formal period of this form of prayer in imitation of the structure of Christian Meditation. This new construct would stand on its own feet and be distinct from the current contemplative forms. Periods of aspiratory prayer could be cultivated each day, of twenty minutes to a half hour in length, with the whole time given over to aspirations. The practice of sensible-spiritual aspirations would likely be more discursive than contemplative, but this admirable beginners' practice would lead into spiritual aspirations and a more contemplative mode. The aspiration could be a mantra, or it could be spontaneous expressions of love and desire. The single mantra is more compatible with a contemplative emphasis than multiple expressions would be.

Whatever the exact structure aspiratory prayer will take, it will usually be pre-fabricated and perfunctory in the beginning. The rote method will soon give way to spontaneity and be part of one's personal approach to God in formal meditations or in diffuse expressions throughout the day. Hopefully aspirations will again be part of a vigorous spirituality for many fervent souls.

Endnotes

1 John Cassian Conference 10: 10. 136 Paulist Press 1985.

2 Laurence Freeman discusses Augustine Baker in his audio series *All and Nothing* tape 5.

3 Philip Sheldrake, "Journey, Spiritual," *The New Westminster Dictionary of Christian Spirituality* (ed. Philip Sheldrake, Louisville: Westminster John Knox Press, 2005) 388-390

4 Aspiratory prayer is more at home with the language of human love than with the intellectual categories of Greek philosophy, which uses contemplation as the highest expression of the love of God. The literature of the Touraine Reform seems to prefer the language of love. One of my esteemed Carmelite teachers and mentors over a lifetime, whose life and studies were dominated by Touraine, frequently showed annoyance at the ambiguities of the vocabulary of contemplation. He preferred to speak of "love" and "loving" as the true measure of prayer rather than contemplation. Instead of describing Carmelite life as "contemplative," he preferred the simple word "prayerful" and the measure of prayer was the depth of love it contained.

5 *Spiritual Direction – Beyond the Beginnings* (New York: Paulist Press, 2000).

6 *Passionate Spirituality, Hildegard of Bingen and Hadewijch of Brabant* (New York: Paulist Press, 2005),

7 Romero de Lima Gouvea, O.Carm., "Vivre d'amour: la priere aspirative chez Therese de l'Enfant Jesus (1873-1897), *Carmelus 47(2000) 19-40*

8 Janssen, 27

9 This is the conclusion of James Walsh, S.J., in his introduction to the Classics of Western Spirituality edition of *The Cloud of Unknowing* (New York: Paulist,1989)

10 Janssen, 210

11 Jean de St. Samson, *L'eguillon, les flames, les fleches, et le miroir de l'amour de Dieu*, in *Oeuvres completes* I, edition critique par Hein Blommestijn (Rome: Institutum Carmelitanum, 1992) 98. Translation my own, from

this first of ten volumes of the critical edition of the works to be published under the direction of Hein Blommestijn, O.Carm.

12 This is the primary application in *The Carmelite Directory of the Spiritual Life* by John Breninger, O.Carm. and in the works of his student, Kilian J. Healy, O.Carm., who presented the topic in his highly regarded *Walking with God* (recently reprinted under the title, *Awakening your Soul to the Presence of God*) and in his *Methods of Prayer. The Carmelite Directory* (tr. Leo J. Walter, O.Carm. Chicago: Carmelite Press, 1951) 471-504. Kilian J. Healy's *Walking with God* is out of print, but *Awakening Your Soul* is available from Manchester, NH: Sophia Institute Press, 1999 and his *Methods of Prayer* (1956) has been reprinted (Roma: Edizioni Carmelitane, 2005) ch. VI. Both Breninger and Healy situate Aspirative prayer, not in the context of love mysticism or passionate spirituality, but as a function of committed friendship with God. As a result they do not stress the emotional or sensible side of the teaching or develop the special mystique of this form of prayer.

Chapter Eight

Christian Mindfulness

There are several classic disciplines in traditional Christian spirituality that cultivate attentiveness and awareness of God and divine things. They are recollection, the practice of the presence of God, and the sacrament of the present moment, all venerable exercises in the Christian life. Recollection, a concept and practice dear to St Teresa of Avila, means in her words that "the soul collects its faculties together and enters within itself to be with its God."[1] She goes on to say that the soul is "centered there within itself." Recollection allows one to meet God in the depths of one's being. The practice of the presence of God is cultivating alertness to one of the many ways God is present and relating to that presence by brief acts of recognition and prayer. The sacrament of the present moment sees each activity in life as an opportunity to meet God. Mindfulness is similar to these three practices, but with its own emphasis. As a Christian practice it is a newcomer on the block. Its name and its particular approach come from the East, particularly from Buddhism. Christian mindfulness adds to God's presence special attention to the concrete and finite aspects of each action.

The present chapter examines Christian mindfulness for the light it throws both on Christian Meditation itself and on conduct between the times of formal meditation. Mindfulness is precisely what we endeavor to do in the practice of Christian Meditation, in which saying the mantra is the prayer. In the rest of the day we cultivate mindfulness to make it a prominent feature of our ongoing consciousness.

The older practices highlight awareness of God's presence and will be a direct line of communication between the person and God. Here lies a possible limitation, which might be called abstractness. It is too easy for the remembrance of God's presence, especially on the run, to be a mere nod of the mind to a theological truth with minimal resonance in one's being. Mindfulness offers the missing piece, namely, a real presence to what one is doing at a given moment.

Mindfulness emphasizes the presence of our total selves in the moment. Actually true recollection demands this too, but the full presence is too easily forgotten. Mindfulness will not let us forget this aspect. So the two disciplines, recollection and mindfulness, together and separately, emphasize full commitment of one's whole being to the moment at hand. They demand the awareness of one's self, the action, and the God who is there. The shorthand for true recollection and Christian mindfulness is presence to the moment, a phrase we hope to elucidate in this book.

Presence to the moment is concentrated or focused attention; it means being "all there". Often we are only half there, present in body but miles away in thought. John of the Cross alludes to a well-known scholastic adage when he writes that "the soul lives where she loves more than in the body she animates."[2] The schoolboy is already out on the playing field as he impatiently looks at the clock and waits for it to strike the end of the school day. In mindfulness we are present in love to what we are actually doing. We are present contemplatively, that is, with our whole person – body, soul and spirit – and not just with our mind or half-hearted will. We do not act absent-mindedly or on automatic pilot. True presence is steady, non-discursive attention, which at the same time is relaxed and self-possessed.

St Therese of Lisieux is a perfect example of mindfulness. According to Ida Goerres she "accomplished the apparently impossible feat of being, every moment, in a state of sharply focused, intensely controlled alertness, and at the same time completely unselfconscious and spontaneous in all that she did."[3] Monica Furlong says that Therese gave up fantasies and impossible dreams in favor of living in the present and making her little acts of love and acceptance. "Her 'Little Way,'" she writes, "was, in some curious way, the reversal of everything she had been taught, the inflated form of Christianity with its dreams of sanctity and martyrdom. Now she saw that all you were asked to do was follow the will of God, whatever it might be, and to give yourself unreservedly to that life and to no other." [4]

Therese, according to her novice mistress, was "mystic, comic, everything... She could make you weep with devotion and just as easily split your sides with laughter during recreation." [5] That is full presence to each changing moment of the day.

Hans Urs von Balthasar concurs with these words about Therese:

> *At each moment, her sole concern is to carry out the will of God as it was revealed to her second to second... Therese never tries to dominate the course of events. In a very womanly fashion, she simply tries to receive everything, and to receive it lovingly. For her, every moment comes so fresh and immediately from the hand of God... [She writes:] "I just keep concentrating on the present moment. I forget the past and preserve myself from worries about the future"* [6]

There are also plenty of examples of the opposite of mindfulness. Here is one example from Tilden Edwards from the comic strip, Calvin and Hobbes.[7] Calvin does not like to relate to real experiences, because they are not clear; they are unpredictable and hard to figure out. He prefers to stay on the outside of things, and that is why he likes life filtered through television. That way he doesn't have to think. He can follow the action with glazed eyes and partial attention. Everything is neat and tidy, but very superficial. Reducing reality in this way is to take the mystery out of life. It is to fail to be fully present to the moment.

Mindlessness is lazy thinking or failure to think at all. It allows one to gloss over things. But if we want to live intentionally with commitment to what we are about, we have to gather up ourselves in recollection and be involved in what we are doing. It is a short step to being in touch with the God hidden in the moment. That is what the Christian practice of recollection and mindfulness attempt to do.

Two entries in Thomas Merton's journals illustrate the contrast between mindfulness and its contrary, mindlessness. They occur at the end of the time he was working through an experience of falling in love with a young woman, the nurse who cared for him in the hospital. He registers in detail the emotional roller coaster he was on over a period of several months. Toward the end of the struggle he made this entry, which is an experience of mindfulness:

> *June 15, 1966... This morning for the first time, really since going to the hospital, I have real inner freedom and solitude – I love M. but in a different way, peacefully and without disturbances or inner tension. I feel that once again I am* ***all here.*** *I have finally returned to my place and to my work, and am beginning once again to be what I am.*[8]

Contrast this presence to himself with the fragmentation a month later, indicating the struggle to deal with his emotions was not over:

> *July 14, 1966...Noted general dispersion and distractedness all yesterday, obviously, [because he had been busy on errands in town] and all night. Only recovered a real awake mindfulness after about 3 hours of reading, etc. this morning. The other state was of an anxious, disoriented consciousness, not properly centered, and making erratic and desperate acts, calling on God, trying to recover orientation, thinking of M., questioning self, fearing consequences of imprudence etc.*[9]

Note how Merton tried to regain mindfulness from his distracted mind by reading, reflection, and no doubt - prayer. The need is to enter into one's self; just being busy is a challenge, but often an excuse for many- mindedness or mindlessness.

Mindfulness is one form of pondering events in the way Mary does in the gospels. It is not enough to be amazed as the shepherds were at Bethlehem. We have to ponder them as Mary did and enter into them, seeking understanding, tuning into the divine presence manifested there. We need to listen with the ear of the heart and sit with mystery. Each moment is a revelation, a unique gift from God. We enter it with wonder and gratefulness and with a receptive heart. This is contemplative living; it is living in God's presence and cultivating the sacrament of the present moment.

Buddhist Mindfulness

Mindfulness has an eastern flavor and is practiced there in various styles of yoga and meditation and martial arts. In its eastern practice it has a different philosophical foundation and different goal from the Christian form. But the Buddhist practice is transferable to a Christian setting by the simple but immensely important addition of the presence of God. In Buddhist mindfulness the only object is to be totally present to what one is doing. It does not make any reference to God, because Buddhism is non-theistic and has no personal God. The Absolute, the God of the Buddhists, is outside their purview of reality; God is totally unknowable, beyond the grasp of the human mind. So Buddhist mindfulness settles for seeking total presence to the moment without distraction or divided attention. We believe that we can learn to be present from this practice, but also to include the dimension of God in the presence. In this way we are baptizing it for Christian usage. We call it Christian mindfulness.

Our standing Christian tradition teaches us to go to God through creation, through the finite and the concrete. All experience of God is mediated. The East can tell us something we always knew. It can help us see our tradition in a new light and realize how important the finite and the concrete are in the spiritual life. We find God by going through the human. It is only a manner of speaking for us to say that we get beyond creatures to find God. Our goal is ultimately the awareness of the Trinity and participation in life with the Father, the Son, and the Holy Spirit. This goal is best served by paying attention to the vehicle that brings us there and that is our created activity. We are helped by being rooted in the existential moment.

We are a sacramental people. The more down-to-earth we are, the more our feet are planted squarely on the ground and the less we fly off in flights of fancy, the closer we are to reality and therefore to God. We are an incarnational people and we believe we find Christ in every crevice of the human condition. Since the Incarnation, and especially since the Resurrection, Christ is at the center of the universe and part of every human action. Listen to these words of Karl Rahner, who puts them in the mouth of Christ: "I am the blind alleys of all your paths, for when you no longer know how to go any further, then you have reached me, foolish child, though you are not aware of it."[10] We find Christ by going through, not around creation. This is to follow what is called the "analogical imagination" by writers like David Tracy, or the "Catholic imagination" by William Lynch, S.J. or Andrew Greeley. Mindfulness helps us reclaim our birthright. The Buddhist teaching on mindfulness can help us see these truths more clearly.

A signature example of the Buddhist mode is washing the dishes when you are washing the dishes. It is the quaint trademark of the Vietnamese Buddhist, Thich Nhat Hanh, in his book, The Miracle of Mindfulness. He writes as follows:

While washing the dishes, you might be thinking about the tea afterwards, and so try to get them out of the way as quickly as possible in order to sit and drink tea. But that means you are incapable of living during the time you are washing the dishes. When you are washing the dishes, washing the dishes must be the most important thing in your life. Just as when you are drinking tea, drinking tea must be the most important thing in your life.[11]

The inner meaning of the Buddha's teaching on mindfulness is found in the Sattipatthanda Sutta and it is summarized in the following words of a Buddhist commentator:

*Mindfulness deepens mental concentration (**samatha**) in the direction of meditation insight (**vipassana**). In mindfulness the disciple dwells in contemplation of the body, feelings and thoughts. Through being concentrated and mindful of these factors of our life, and by clearly comprehending through insight their true nature, the world of hate and greed, of sorrow and grief, is overcome and **Nibbana** [nirvana] is attained.*[12] ***Samatha** and **vipassana** describe two different kinds of Buddhist meditation, the former seeking tranquility and the latter insight.*[13] *Both goals are the fruit of total presence. Listen to Nhat Hanh's description of washing the dishes: "While washing the dishes one should only be washing the dishes, which means that while washing the dishes one should be completely aware of the fact that one is washing the dishes."*[14]

The total presence is the heart of meditation in the East. A similar presence, but with the addition of a Trinitarian component, is the goal of Christian Meditation as taught by John Main. When I engage in the practice of Christian Meditation, I do not imagine God or anything else. I simply try to be totally present to my deepest self and to the God who dwells there. To the extent that I am successful, I am giving my full focused attention to my interior being and to the Trinity. I am not thinking about God or about anything. I am practicing contemplation, that is, I am in communion with the real and the Real. It is important to know that John Main does not equate contemplation with a special psychological experience of God. Contemplation for him is an existential act; it is participation or communion with God. In true mindfulness I am acting out of the spirit level of my being and I am truly free and loving. I touch both the reality of God and my own deepest reality.

Free and loving presence to the present moment is the essence of contemplation, mindfulness and meditation. You wash the dishes to wash the dishes, intentionally and with as little distraction as possible, not to impress your neighbor or even to provide clean dishes. These motives are extraneous and pertain to the future. You want to stay in the now. To accomplish that you need to be present to yourself. Here is a wise story from Mobi Ho, the translator of *The Miracle of Mindfulness*. She recalls in the preface an incident when she was cooking furiously and she had to stop and search for a missing spoon. She was obviously agitated. Thay came into the room and smiled and said; "What is Mobi looking for?" "The spoon," she answered, perhaps a bit petulantly. Thay answered with another smile: "No, Mobi is looking for Mobi."[15]

Why Mindfulness is Important

Our distractions come from our divided and disordered selves. Our desires are the product of our many-mindedness, and this in turn comes from our lack of integration. Our desires need to be integrated with our whole person and with what we are about at the moment. Our thought needs to be one-pointed and simple, an accomplishment that takes practice, discipline and grace.

Practice in meditation and in mindfulness will develop the virtues needed and give me a handle on my desires. Perfect mindfulness will neutralize the warring factions within me and let me be absorbed by what I am doing. In this latter case I will have achieved what the psychologists call the de-automatization of my desires. This means that I have neutralized the impulses and desires I do not want. Instead I can concentrate on my true wishes. The unwanted desires dry up and atrophy for lack of nurture.[16] From a moral or spiritual point of view I have let my faith inform and animate all my behavior. I have attained true freedom and perfect love. I have achieved what John Cassian called purity of heart.

Nhat Hahn celebrates the personal freedom in mindful activity in these words:

> *The fact that I am standing there and washing these bowls is a wondrous reality. I am being completely myself, following my breath, conscious of my presence, and conscious of my thoughts and actions. There is no way I can be tossed around mindlessly like a bottle slapped here and there on the waves.*[17]

The Christian adds the further element of the good intention and remembering God's presence. I am present to God and receiving the impact of his presence, which is a fact before and after I am aware of it. I do not constitute that presence. I am alive with the presence of God. This aspect is not something extraneous and accidental. It belongs to the nature of things, to the immanence of God in all of creation. God's delight is to be with the children of this world, in our sorrow and in our own delights. This presence is for our sakes and our salvation.

Christians emphasize the presence of God in all things, but they may tend to forget the envelope that contains it. Persons, actions, events are the medium through which God comes. The given moment is the only place one can meet God. In God there is no time, only the eternal now. God lives in that now moment on the other side of the veil that separates time from eternity. We enter the vestibule of that "now," when we concentrate on the present moment. Our beloved God is there, and it behooves us to be there as well. To enter the now moment is to let anxiety fall off our shoulders and to be renewed in hope by touching the God who loves us.

The more that a person possesses herself, the more present she can be. She must be "all there", alert, aware, attentive, in a word, fully present. Intellectualizing or head knowledge are of little value. An abstract recall or thinking about God's presence in the here and now is not enough. The knowledge must be holistic and experiential, beyond mere thinking, beyond mind alone. What we need is heart knowledge. I am more than my thoughts or my mind, and therefore I must not identify with my mind or my ego.

In mindfulness we stand before the Lord, "watching and waiting." We do not control the relationship, and we are there to receive a gift. Every moment is a gift from God and we are aware of that fact. Every moment can be an occasion of contemplation, i.e. an opportunity to realize God's love. The contemplative walks in the presence of God in a moment to moment experience of God's love. The condition for the gift is to be present there, body, soul and spirit.

Mindfulness fights the enemies of wholeness and cultivates full presence to God. The enemies of wholeness are what divide us, such as our addictions and compulsions, our un-freedoms and attachments, our sins and imperfections. They undermine our love of God. Mindfulness faces these temptations head on by maintaining attention to the call of faith. We are thoroughly present to the moment, because it is God's call for us at that time. Mindfulness recognizes distractions, calls them by name, then lets them pass, all the while gently focusing on the moment.

As focused or non-discursive attention, mindfulness helps us rise above what John Main calls the "monkey chatter" of the distracted mind. When we are mindless we are un-rooted and un-centered, we flit about from one distraction to another, dissipating our energies, prisoners of unrecognized consumerism and self-glorification. When we are mindless we live outside ourselves and engage only the part of ourselves that is needed to satisfy each passing whim. We are dilettantes and escapists and have no depth or solid ground within ourselves on which to rest commitments. When we are mindless we are more vulnerable to the winds of change around us and easily give way to worry and anxiety, simply because we don't realize that "God is near." (Phil 4.5)

Excessive "busyness" is lack of mindfulness. Busyness is a cultural demon of our time that none of us are immune from, often a way of avoiding what we are really called to do. It can be an escape from the real demands of relationships and often an excuse for not giving time to that primary relationship of our lives, being with God. Busyness is a wolf in sheep's clothing, because it looks like virtue but actually covers a whole array of self-interest. Even charity can be done as an ego trip. Look more closely at its manifestations and you will find a driven and compulsive spirit that hurts one's health, peace of mind, and awareness of others. Over-busy persons are trying to prove themselves by the sheer quantity of their output. The more they do, the more they feed their self-satisfaction and basking in the imagined plaudits of the multitude. There is little charity in this addiction, appearances to the contrary notwithstanding. The motivation in busyness is ego-enhancement, the desire to impress, even to show up the neighbor. Busyness is ersatz zeal; we all need to be mindful of our motivation.

The basic reason why mindfulness is good and its opposite bad is because one is the expression of the true self, and the other the offspring of the false self. The true self comes from the deeper strata of our being, from our spirit, and it carries body and psyche with it. Thus it incarnates more of ourselves in its choices than does the splintered false self. The true self acts from the heart and not from self-deception or free-floating emotions. It acts virtuously because it is rooted in God.

The ego-centered self is also known as the 'false self' because it is not really who we are. Theologically it is the result of original sin; a sort of self-consciousness and judgment that doesn't allow us to be spontaneous and free. Psychologically it is the constructed self, conditioned by our experiences from the past. In many ways self-centering comes about through fear. It comes out of primitive experiences of life that set in place ways of coping with threats to one's security or self-importance.

The sense of individual self is not bad in itself, we need an ego in order to act and present a persona to the world, but it needs to open to others in love and charity. Redemption in the Christian tradition is precisely this turning outward in love. But psychology will tell us that we are only able to do this, only able to love, when we ourselves feel loved, when we feel safe. The Christian revelation is that we are infinitely loved and cared for; "every hair of our head has been numbered". The ego-self, constructed from the pains of the past, needs to be held in love and forgiveness and as we learn to forgive others we discover that we are forgiven. It is this experience of being loved by God that enables us to love God in return, and others in God. The ego is redeemed, put at the service of charity; it serves rather than seeks to be served. In these cases the true self has taken over, original spontaneity has been restored. The Holy Spirit has become the fountain of living water springing up to eternal life (John 4:14 and John 7:36-37). Mindfulness is a sign that love is doing its work of integration.

One important final question is the practice: how do I become more mindful? The answer is: cultivate a vibrant spiritual life. Mindfulness is a by-product of mature holiness. But are there special means for growing in the practice and skill? How can I become more mindful?

I want to suggest two special means. One is meditation itself, the other the basic condition of all prayer, purity of heart. These are the two arms for embracing God and will bring us to mindfulness.

First, mindfulness is the outcome of faithfulness to the two periods of Christian Meditation each day, since meditation itself is explicit and prolonged mindfulness. Practice makes perfect; obviously meditation will foster the habit of mindfulness. Conventional wisdom says: find God in daily prayer and you will find God everywhere. The Sufi came out of his prayer room and said: I went to the marketplace and found God everywhere. The contrary is also true: without regular meditation it is much harder to find God. General mindfulness throughout the day is a diffuse presence to God. How could this be maintained, if it is not nourished by a focused or concentrated presence? How to be mindful of God in the comings and goings of the day, if one never takes time to meet God face to face? We need to focus on the Lord, to come aside and find rest for our souls. Otherwise we will not recognize God when he appears in the disguise of other people or works of charity.

The two periods of Christian Meditation come from a long tradition. One of the outstanding teachers of recollection, the contemporary and early teacher of St. Teresa of Avila, Francis of Osuna, recommended two periods of formal meditation a day, each of them an hour's length. Osuna writes: "You are to retire into your heart and leave all created things for the length of two hours, one hour before and the other after noon, at the most quiet time possible." [18] During the rest of the day the mind is to be occupied with *lectio divina,* the author agreeing with St. Bonaventure that "no one can call himself devoted to the sacred passion unless he spends most of [the day] contemplating it in one manner or another."[19] The two hours a day suggested by Osuna may be beyond the possibilities for many people, and periods of twenty to thirty minutes have proved workable for most people today. *Lectio Divina* is not just scripture reading but reading the presence of God at all times in our life; in our work, in our relationships, in the world around us. So it is possible!

The second way to cultivate mindfulness is purity of heart. It is as important as formal prayer, because the measure of one's purity of heart is the measure of one's prayer. Again this is the constant teaching of the Christian tradition from John Cassian to Teilhard de Chardin. What is purity of heart? It is detachment, and specifically, affective detachment. This is the freedom of the will before choices. This freedom is cultivated especially by effective detachment, renouncing whatever stands in the way to one's service of God. Affective detachment comes from effective detachment.

In the western tradition renunciation is the way to recollection. Writers like Francis of Osuna, Teresa of Avila, and John of the Cross underline the gospel teaching that we must leave all things to follow the Lord. A recent exponent of this age-old tradition is Pope Benedict XVI, who put the teaching in fresh language to his interviewer, Peter Seewald, shortly before the death of John Paul II: "When it comes down to it," Cardinal Ratzinger said, "everyone has to under go his own Exodus. He not only has to leave the place that nurtured him and become independent, but has to come out of his own reserved self. He must leave himself behind, transcend his own limits; only then will he reach the Promised Land, so to speak."[20]

Christian teachers generally emphasize the physical renunciation of legitimate goods and pleasures, such as marriage or possessions or worldly honors; they call for the renunciation of all desires. These are refrains in their writing, and modern readers are easily put off by such total demands. But contemporary readers need to be reminded that these classic directives are always in the context of God's will and the journey of discovering who we are in God. God does have a particular will for each person, it is particular because it is to become the unique person that we really are. The freedom to be the person that we are called to be is the controlling factor for renouncing goods. What is renounced is what impairs our freedom, our disordered desires, those that block the spirit's action in our lives. Hence the need for purity of heart – to let God work in us.

The wholesale rejection of desires therefore applies to disordered desires. Discernment helps us to sense what is an impulse of the spirit of love and what is the grasping of the ego. The Christian criterion for choices is; are we acting out of freedom and expansion of spirit, or are we acting out of fear and self-protection. Or, putting it even more simply; are we thinking about ourselves or are we letting go of self-preocupation so that we can become the spontaneous person that we are.

The language in this tradition can betray us. Osuna, for example, presents recollection as involving the transcending or going beyond all creatures. The person must be "blind, deaf and dumb to everything that is not God." We need to "guard the heart with all vigilance, unburdening and clearing it of all created things, so that the one who created it may emerge with the life of grace."[21] The cost of divine union is "not less than everything." The sweeping language might make one think that the whole of creation must be rejected. Not so, these authors tell us. The everything to be bypassed is the all that is in competition or opposed to God.

The teaching on recollection attributes the same high efficacy as mindfulness, but also makes the same demands for its functioning. Karl Rahner in an essay on the Holy Eucharist says that recollection demands letting go of all false and harmful things.[22] The teaching is founded on the Paschal Mystery, the death and resurrection of the Lord, which is "the innermost law of our lives." Baptism initiates us into this mystery and the Holy

Eucharist renews the commitment. Eucharistic life, he writes, embraces the total profane life of the Christian, the "everyday" of the followers of Jesus. We die and rise with Jesus Christ, not only at Mass and in Holy Communion, but in our everyday behavior.

How can we manage so sublime a calling? Rahner's answer is recollection, which he defines as "withdrawing into ourselves" and from there making the right choices at each moment. Withdrawing into ourselves is not copping out or fleeing the scene. It is being our true selves and living intentionally. Get beyond the distractions, turn off the constant radio, stop the "empty talk and gossip," avoid wasting time with worthless reading, and pull back from the "over-busy and all devouring fulfillment of one's duty... (the busyness which is) an excuse for avoiding our real duty."[23] Enter into yourselves, so that you are your true selves.

Recollection is no flight from life, but "facing up to ourselves as we really are, confronting ourselves instead of seeking solace in chatter, conversations, mere external dissipations"[24] Holy Communion commits me to "accept my everyday just as it is. I do not need to have any lofty feelings in my heart to recount... I can lay my everyday before [God] just as it is,.. in all its pettiness and triviality".[25] Christian recollection is another word for Christian mindfulness, and these two are at the heart of our search for God that is anchored in the two daily periods of contemplative prayer that is Christian Meditation.

Endnotes

1 *The Way of Perfection* 28.4

2 *Spiritual Canticle B*, 5.3

3 Cited from *The Hidden Face* by John Donohue, S.J. in "Therese of Lisieux, Doctor of the Church," *America*, 177 (December 13, 1997) 16

4 *Therese of Lisieux* (New York:Pantheon, 1987) 96

5 Cited in Donohue, 16

6 *Two Sisters in the Spirit: Therese of Lisieux and Elizabeth of the Trinity* (tr. Donald Nichols and Ann Elizabeth Englund, San Francisco: Ignatius Press, 1970) 66-67.

7 "Valuing the Living Moment," *Shalem News*, cited in *Kinospirit* (November, 1995) 2

8 Learning to Love, the Journals of Thomas Merton 6(ed. Christine M. Bochen, San Francisco:Harper, 1997) 84

9 *Ibid.* 95.

10 *The Great Church Year, the Best of Karl Rahner's Homilies, Sermons and Meditations* (ed. Albert Raffelt, New York:Crossroad, 1993) 51

11 Boston: Beacon Press, 1987, 24

12 Ven Dr. Dhammarakkhita, "Mindfulness and Loving-Kindness Meditation," *The Gethsemani Encounter* (eds. Donald W. Mitchell and James A. Wiseman, O.S.B., New York: Continuum, 1998)35-41, at 35

13 William Rehg, S.J., *Christian Mindfulness, Studies in the Spirituality of the Jesuits,* 34/3 (May, 2005) 5-9.

14 *Ibid.*3

15 *Ibid.* x

16 Philip Novak, "The Practice of Attention," *Parabola* 15(May, 1990)10-12, citing the seminal article by Arthur J. Deikman, "Deautomatization and the Mystic Experience", *Psychiatry* 29 (1966) 324-338.

17 Op.cit, 4

18 *The Third Spiritual Alphabet, Classics of Western Spirituality* (tr. Mary E. Giles, New York: Paulist Press, 1981) 388.

19 *Ibid.* 177

20 Paul Elie, "The Year of Two Popes," *Atlantic Monthly*, 297(January-February, 2006)71.

21 Op.cit, 132

22 "The Eucharist and Our Daily Lives," *Theological Investigations, 7* (*tr* David Bourke, New York: Herder and Herder, 1971) 211-226

23 *Ibid, 221*

24 *Ibid*, 222

25 *Ibid*, 222

Biographical Note of Author
Ernest E. Larkin, O.Carm.
1922-2006

Ernest E. Larkin, O.Carm., was born in Chicago, on August 19, 1922, and entered the Carmelite minor seminary in 1935, pursuing the formation and studies program in the Order until ordination to the priesthood in 1946. He did graduate work in Rome, at St. Thomas University, from 1948 to 1950 and obtained the doctorate in theology (STD) in 1954. Besides two years as a high school teacher his first twenty years of ministry were spent teaching in the Carmelite major seminary in Washington, D.C., in the 50s and at The Catholic University of America in the 60s. In 1970 he went to Phoenix, Arizona, and worked in continuing education of the clergy for two years, at the end of which he helped found the Kino Institute, a diocesan, adult education center for theology and ministry. In the 1980s and 1990s he traveled extensively, giving retreats and seminars, concentrating on Carmelite spirituality and contemplative prayer. He has been an active teacher and participant in local ministry in Phoenix for many years. Fr. Larkin is remembered as a beloved teacher and friend by all those who knew him.

For further information about the author the reader is invited to consult the chapter, "A Modern Pioneer in Carmelite Spirituality, Ernest E. Larkin, O.Carm." in *Carmelite Prayer, a Tradition for the 21st Century* by Keith J. Egan (New York: Paulist Press 2003) 223-238 and to visit the website **http://carmelnet.org/larkin/larkin.html** to review his published articles.

Active Prayer/ Recollection also known as Acquired Contemplation

Term used by St Teresa and John of the Cross to describe the part human effort plays in contemplation, the gathering of the mind around a focal point of image or word. What John Main calls the 'work', the 'discipline' of meditation.

Passive Prayer/ Infused contemplation

Term used by Teresa and John to describe the part grace plays in drawing the mind into God. At this point, like St Paul, "we do not know how to pray but the Spirit prays within us in groans that cannot be put into words".

Centering/ Centering Prayer

Method that combines active and passive recollection taught by Contemplative Outreach, especially Thomas Keating O.C.S.O. and Basil Pennington O.C.S.O.

Christian Meditation

Parallel disciple taught by John Main O.S.B. and Laurence Freeman O.S.B. involving the use of a Mantra.

Contemplation/ Meditation

Synonymous terms. In the past 'meditation' was used in the Christian tradition to describe reflection on scriptural passages, now, in dialogue with religions that had their origin in India, it is understood to have a non-discursive dimension. Meditation is both active and passive.

Mental / Discursive Prayer

'Active' prayer that uses the human faculties of memory, understanding and will. A 'subject' or scriptural passage is chosen to reflect on, a moral extracted and then applied in one's life. Also known as 'prayer of acts' that followed the stages: Reflection, Petition/Intercession, Adoration and Application.

Ignatian Prayer Prayer taught in the Spiritual Exercises of St Ignatius that encourages the use of the imagination so as to 'enter into' scriptural passages. Modern commentaries on the Exercises show that the use of imagination does not preclude but should lead to the imageless form of contemplation.

Liturgy Communal prayer of the Church, especially Mass and the use of the Psalter in morning and evening prayer.

Devotions Personal prayer to particular saints or aspects of Divine revelation. The Rosary for example is a devotion that often leads to contemplation in a similar way as the repetition of a prayer phrase. Modern use of the rosary however tends to stress reflection on 'the mysteries'.

Lectio Divina Monastic tradition of prayerful reading of a scriptural passage where the text is 'chewed over' so as to center the mind until a phrase or word begins to speak to the heart. This in turn can lead into Contemplation/meditation.

Cataphatic Prayer using images or thoughts about God. Theology based on what we can say about God also known as via positiva.

Apophatic Prayer without thoughts or images. That aspect of theology which says that God is not this, not that, the way of unknowing. Also known as the via negativa.

Mindfulness Term taken from Buddhism that means attentiveness, awareness of what you are doing and what is going on inside you. Could also be paralleled with 'recollection', 'the practice of the presence of God' and 'the sacrament of the present moment' in the Christian tradition.